Praise f

"Use this wonderful book as a guide on :
deeply engage your workforce and build enduring trust.

—From the foreword by Stephen M. R. Covey,
NY Times Best-Selling Author of *The Speed of Trust*

"7 Lenses is a CEO must-read for gaining a fresh perspective on ethical leadership and what it can mean to the success of your organization."

—**Chip Conley**, Founder, Joie de Vivre Hospitality and Fest300
and *NY Times* Best-Selling Author of *Emotional Equations*

"Oscar & Felix, Laurel & Hardy, Marilyn Monroe & Arthur Miller—odd couples or matches made in heaven? In her new book, 7 Lenses, Linda Fisher Thornton challenges us to take a deeper look at how ethics and leadership not only go well together but also are inextricably connected to the other's success."

—**Marshall Goldsmith**, the Thinkers50 Award Winner
(sponsored by *Harvard Business Review*) for Most Influential
Leadership Thinker in the World

"This book is a thought-provoking look at ethical responses to leadership challenges. I highly recommend it as a tool for having meaningful discussions with leaders in your organization."

—**Dr. Mark Goulston, M.D.**, Co-Founder of Heartfelt Leadership
and Author of International Best-Seller *Just Listen*

"Trustworthy and ethical behavior is the foundation for lasting leadership success. In 7 Lenses, Linda Fisher Thornton gives leaders a road map to understand and apply the principles that lead to true leadership excellence."

—**Randy Conley**, Trust Practice Leader, The Ken Blanchard Companies

"7 Lenses paints a clear picture of what leaders need to consider in order to make decisions that are best for their organizations and right for society."

—**Paul Klein**, Founder and President, Impakt

"Thank you, Linda! It's about time we get past the simplistic rule-based do's and don'ts approach to ethics that ties us in can't-win knots. 7 Lenses offers just the type of principle-based ethics leaders can use to take responsibility for the greatest number of wins across diverse contexts."

—**Christopher Avery**, Founder and President, Partnerwerks, Inc.

"Without ethics, the actions of business soon become a heartless game and can do more harm than good. With a focus on ethics, the best of the best will rise even further, and this wonderful book will guide them."

—**Juliet Funt**, Founder/CEO WhiteSpace

"Linda has nicely laid the steps to win without taking any shortcuts. It is one of those books that should be required reading for any leader or any professional who aspires to be a leader."

—**Rajesh Setty**, Serial Entrepreneur and Business Alchemist, RajeshSetty.com

"I appreciate a business book that discusses not only how to improve business but also how to build a better world. Well done, Linda."

—**Keith Ferrazzi**, NY Times Best-Selling Author of Who's Got Your Back?

"In our interdependent world, the ability to trust one another is critical. The proactive strategies in 7 Lenses provide a working framework for becoming ethical leaders and creating an ethical culture—the type of culture that will drive our collaboration economy."

—**Eric Lowitt**, Author of The Collaboration Economy

"Like mom and apple pie, we all agree in principle as to what 'it is' when it comes to ethical leadership. Linda frames it in such a way that enables us to practice ethical leadership on a daily basis. I think it's the first book that is so focused on the application, and that makes it a must-read for everyone in business and not."

—**Peter Winick**, Founder/CEO, Thought Leadership Leverage

"7 Lenses describes the future of ethical leadership in vivid detail and guides us in how to implement it in day-to-day decisions and actions."

—**Barbara Kimmel**, Executive Director, Trust Across America - Trust Around the World, and Editor of Trust Inc.: Strategies for Building Your Company's Most Valuable Asset

"The 7 Lenses approach to ethical leadership provides valuable frameworks revealing required lifelong learning for making successful positive personal and organizational difference. A welcomed addition to every leader's bookshelf."

—**Steven N. Pyser**, Assistant Professor, Fox School of Business, Temple University; Caux Round Table Fellow

"Linda Fisher Thornton's 7 Lenses gives leaders a practical and much-needed guidebook to making better choices in an increasingly complex world. I highly recommend adding it to your leadership library and, more importantly, using it as a discussion starter in your organization. We all need it."

—**Karlin Sloan**, CEO, Karlin Sloan & Company, and Author of Smarter, Faster, Better, Unfear, and Lemonade: The Leader's Guide to Resilience at Work

LENSES

LENSES

LEARNING ᴛʜᴇ PRINCIPLES
ᴀɴᴅ PRACTICES ᴏꜰ
ETHICAL LEADERSHIP

LINDA FISHER THORNTON

FOREWORD BY STEPHEN M. R. COVEY

LEADING IN CONTEXT LLC
RICHMOND, VA

LEADING INCONTEXT

Published by
Leading in Context LLC
Richmond, VA
www.LeadinginContext.com

Publisher's Cataloging-in-Publication Data
Thornton, Linda Fisher.

    7 lenses : learning the principles and practices of ethical leadership / Linda Fisher Thornton ; foreword by Stephen M. R. Covey. – Richmond, VA : Leading in Context LLC, 2013.

    p. ; cm.

    ISBN13: 978-1-936662-11-1

    1. Business ethics. 2. Leadership—Moral and ethical aspects. 3. Industrial management—Moral and ethical aspects. I. Title. II. Covey, Stephen M. R.

    HF5387.T46 2013
    174.4-dc23   2013948162

A Leading in Context LLC Book

FIRST EDITION

Project coordination by Jenkins Group, Inc.
www.BookPublishing.com

Cover design by Chris Rhoads
Interior design by Brooke Camfield

Printed in the United States of America
17   16   15   14   13   •   5   4   3   2   1

This book is dedicated to all leaders who seek to make a positive difference in lives, organizations, communities, and the world.

To seek the highest good is to live well.

—Saint Augustine

*Act that your principle of action might
safely be made a law for the whole world.*

—Immanuel Kant

*Trust and confidence sustain free markets and ethical business
practices provide the basis for such trust and confidence.*

—Caux Roundtable Principles for Responsible Business

*Classic economic theory, based as it is on an inadequate
theory of human motivation, could be revolutionized
by accepting the reality of higher human needs, including the
impulse to self-actualization and the love for the highest values.*

—Abraham Maslow

Common ethical ground? I would say so! Teachable? Certainly!

—Dr. Rushworth Kidder

Contents

Foreword

Having helped leaders build trust in organizations worldwide for over twenty years, I see daily just how vitally important ethical choices are. We live in a world where interdependence and connection are our new reality. Our global future depends on our ability to collaborate and partner in new ways and across traditional boundaries. Indeed, trust is the very currency of this collaborative economy, and the foundation of trust is ethics. The more we understand this new reality of global connectedness, the more important ethics becomes.

As founding members of the *Trust Across America Alliance of Trustworthy Business Experts*, Linda and I are part of a global group working together to help build trustworthy behavior in business. When we first met, I told her how important I thought her work was—creating clarity around leading with ethics in a low-trust world. While ethics has always been a difficult subject to discuss, it is also one that is at the very foundational roots of our leadership. We ignore it at our peril. The big and small choices that we make every day as leaders have a profound "ripple effect"—not only on ourselves but especially on all those around us and ultimately even on society. It is our responsibility as leaders to make sure that our impact is positive and mutually beneficial for all stakeholders. That's what leaders do—they get results *in a way* that inspires trust. *How we do what we do* makes all the difference—not only in the outcome, but also in the culture.

This book meets an urgent need by providing a clear, detailed roadmap for ethical leadership. There are plenty of books that approach ethical leadership at the theoretical level. What Linda has done in *7 Lenses* is to develop a practical, actionable model that managers and leaders can use as a guide to make ethical choices in becoming ethical leaders.

I think this book is a clear winner for several reasons. Let me mention just three. First, it insightfully pulls together the bigger picture of what ethical responsibility includes and at the same time provides enough detail to guide our daily actions as leaders. Second, it instructively takes a long-term view of our leadership impact and is steeped in how to build trust at many levels. Finally, it holistically paints a clear picture of the kind of leadership we need in our connected, interdependent world.

Establishing and growing trust with all stakeholders simultaneously is the key leadership competency for success in a connected, interdependent society. This book guides us in how to honor—and build trust with—multiple stakeholders in our daily choices. In *The Speed of Trust: The One Thing That Changes Everything*, I described five waves of trust rippling from the inside out, from self trust to societal trust. I believe that the principles and practices described in this book will help leaders build the kind of trust that brings out the best in themselves and their organizations and that will ultimately ripple out in building broader trust in a global marketplace and in society at large.

I firmly believe that ethical leadership is about congruence and not compliance, about doing what's right rather than merely following the rules. *7 Lenses* makes this distinction clearly and lays out an action plan for implementing congruent leadership personally, in relationships with others, and in society.

Linda's message is simple and clear: ethical leadership not only produces results but it also transforms leaders, organizations, and communities. Use this wonderful book as a guide on your ethical leadership journey, and you will deeply engage your workforce and build enduring trust. As you read this book and, most importantly, apply its principles, I believe you will be inspired to see that there is no limit to what people and organizations led by ethical leaders can accomplish.

—Stephen M. R. Covey

Preface

In writing this book, I seek to clarify what it means to think beyond ourselves. There is an urgent need for clarity about this in the world today, because decisions based only on profit and convenience do not lead us to a better world. It's time for us to talk openly about our responsibilities to current and future generations and how we will fulfill them. In *7 Lenses*, I advocate leadership grounded in respect and care and present a framework for thinking about ethical leadership in seven dimensions of responsibility.

This book is designed to be a guide for learning how to lead ethically for the long term. It offers a common framework for talking about ethical responsibility and is written for leaders who want to build ethical companies and cultures, for leaders who want to create great places to work, and for those who want to learn how to build a better world.

The Origins of This Book

I had been developing leaders for more than twenty-five years and teaching leadership for nine years when I attending an ethics symposium at the University of Richmond. I listened as global experts from a variety of disciplines shared their perspectives on leading for the greater good. They all advocated the highest level of ethical leadership, and their perspectives were compelling, but I was left with some deep questions:

- *Why do intelligent people define ethical responsibility in leadership in so many different ways?*
- *How can we expect people to lead ethically if we can't even agree on what that means?*
- *How can we make sense of all the different perspectives to get a clear picture of the whole?*

Following my curiosity, I looked for a practical framework that pulled all of the perspectives together. Not finding one, I began writing this book. My formal training in linguistics, communications, and adult education and human development led me to use a learning perspective and to explore my questions in the context of human development. I began to sketch a list of practical ethical principles that could guide leaders, and with the support of my mother and mentor Mary Alice Fisher, an expert on ethics in psychology, I began to create a practical framework that represented ethical leadership in a global society.

It became clear to me early in the process of writing this book that the answers to my questions would only come from a viewpoint that looked across traditional schools of thought. While researching across disciplines, I stayed grounded in the timeless wisdom of the ethicists and philosophers whose quotes appear in this book.

In the first two years, I struggled with which principles to include and how to group them. After the principles were finalized, it took many tries to create clear and actionable graphics and a framework for pulling all of the perspectives together into a meaningful whole. Creating the 7 Lenses™ and the four-quadrant matrix of principles that honor them took four years.

How *7 Lenses* Is Organized

This book is organized in three parts, each with an introduction. Part One answers the question "What is ethical leadership" from varying perspectives to get a clear picture of its breadth and depth. Ethical leadership is approached from a learning perspective, as a business advantage, and from seven very different perspectives on ethical responsibility that together form a multidimensional model.

Part Two explores how to honor all 7 Lenses in daily leadership. It introduces a four-quadrant model and 14 Guiding Principles that honor all 7 Lenses. Each chapter includes vivid detail and examples that help guide daily leadership choices.

Part Three explores how ethical expectations are changing. It examines how our understanding of the purpose of leadership is evolving and describes six connected trends shaping the future. Thought-provoking questions in this section help leaders plan for and adapt to changes that are happening now.

People I Would Like to Thank

This book could not have happened without the support and guidance of some wonderful people whom I would like to thank. I extend my gratitude to Mary Alice Fisher, Ph.D., my mentor, mother, and friend, who shared her writing and ethics wisdom with me, struggled through important questions with me, shared research sources and wrote with me, edited the book with me, and gave unending moral support; my husband Joe, who believed in this project and who patiently helped me make this book better through editing and advice; and my children, for providing moral support during the writing of this book and for sharing my enthusiasm for learning and leadership.

I would like to thank Stephen M. R. Covey, Co-founder and Global Practice Leader of the FranklinCovey Speed of Trust Practice, for graciously agreeing to write the Foreword for this book. It is a particular honor for me, since I have learned so much from his writing and speaking about building trust in leadership.

In addition, I would like to thank Peter Winick, my strategy coach, for pushing me to be better and bolder and for helping me clarify my message; the University of Richmond Donchian Symposium on Ethics that stimulated the questions that resulted in this book; Jim Narduzzi, dean of the University of Richmond School of Professional and Continuing Studies, for inviting me to join the adjunct faculty to teach leadership; my leadership students for asking hard questions and taking the intentional journey to better leadership; Dr. Fred Antczak, my dean and advisor at the University of Virginia, who encouraged me to stretch and supported me in developing good thinking and clear communication; and many authors whose work helped shape my thinking about leadership including Dr. Stephen Covey, Howard Gardner, Mark Gerzon, Marshall Goldsmith, Jim Kouzes, Patrick Lencioni, John Maxwell, Peter Senge, Margaret Wheatley, and others who are mentioned in this book.

I am grateful for the support of friends and neighbors who encouraged me to keep writing; people across disciplines who gave positive feedback on social media channels; Jerry Jenkins, Leah Nicholson, Yvonne Roehler, and the rest of the team at the Jenkins Group, who worked their magic and turned a manuscript into a book; and reviewers who suggested improvements, including Kevin Bruny, Karen Conrad, Dr. Chris Lee, Steve Lux, Kathleen McSweeney, Dr. Jim Noland, and Dr. Jake Noland.

Part 1

What is Ethical Leadership?

Have you ever noticed how difficult it is for us to agree on "the right thing" to do? Imagine being part of a leadership team deciding how to handle an ethical dilemma. One leader argues that our impact on people is paramount in making the decision. Another voice reminds us to carefully follow the law. A person in the back of the room says softly, "What about the legacy we're leaving for our children and grandchildren?" Another insists, "We still have to make a profit somehow!"

I believe the reason we don't yet have one commonly shared definition of ethical leadership is that we interpret ethical leadership through different lenses that reflect varying levels of responsibility. It's as if we are standing together close to a mosaic, each describing different individually colored tiles, while missing the beauty of the picture they create. This book is about the broader picture those tiles create.

The ethical leadership described in this book transcends factions, geographic boundaries, and individual values. It reflects the broad-ranging ethics that I believe is necessary in a global society, the kind that builds successful businesses and communities. It considers the complexity of business and our global economy and how our thinking impacts our ethical decisions. It is future focused, describing where ethical leadership is headed, not merely where it has been.

This book clearly describes the ethical leadership that will bring out our best and transform our organizations. Its focus is on how individuals learn and do ethical leadership rather than on philosophical questions about competing branches of ethics. A learning perspective helps "cut through the noise" to answer the burning questions that business leaders struggle with in learning how to lead responsibly. In Part One, I explore ethical leadership as a learning journey and a business advantage and describe it in multiple dimensions I call the 7 Lenses of Ethical Responsibility.

1

A Learning Journey

Moral excellence comes about as a result of habit.
We become just by doing just acts, temperate by doing
temperate acts, brave by doing brave acts.

—Aristotle

The journey to ethical leadership is a learning journey, one that takes us through a highly complex array of situations and challenges. Even with a roadmap to guide us, we can never expect to arrive at our destination because of ever-increasing complexity and change. Several challenges combine in ways that make our progress toward ethical leadership difficult. You may have already encountered these challenges on your learning journey.

Challenges on the Journey to Ethical Leadership

On our journey to ethical leadership, we deal with a complexity of information that is expanding exponentially. Responsible leadership requires thinking on multiple levels at the same time and balancing seemingly competing demands. As we sift through mountains of information, synthesis is required to discover hidden meaning. Through it all, we need to consider the ethical implications of every decision we make in every context.

As members of a global society, we are required to use a global world view and cultural sensitivity. The days of operating in a bubble with things the way "they've always been" are long over. While honoring diverse people and cultures, we must also demonstrate environmental and resource stewardship that anticipates the long-term impact of our work on society and the planet.

To keep up with the pace of change, including trends that cross traditional work boundaries, we must be flexible, agile, and resilient. In the midst of constant change, we must deal effectively with uncertainty and adapt quickly as industries, partnerships, and information change. Only when we continually learn and develop as leaders can we possibly navigate the hurdles and pitfalls on this ethical leadership journey.

No reference book holds the answers to our daily dilemmas—we must find ethical solutions on our own. John C. Knapp, describing the layered complexity of the problems faced by today's leaders, comments that "It will be necessary for groups to cooperate across layers of social organization—across government, business, civil society and academia. No single layer can respond fully."[1]

While business leaders try to keep up with the complexity of work, consumers are paying more attention to the ethical choices they make. Savvy and aware consumers are making more responsible buying choices, sending the message to businesses that ethics matters. They are looking for ethics beyond simple compliance and telling the truth to include reducing environmental impact, ensuring fair labor, and treating customers and employees with respect.

Social connectedness increases awareness of the global context, which increases expectations for demonstrating a global world view.

The broader scope, the constant change, and the increasing visibility of ethical leadership all combine to leave us feeling unsure of our choices. I believe that most leaders want to lead responsibly, but they don't always know exactly what that means.

The Inherent Complexity of Ethical Leadership

In spite of many differences in perspective, there is broad agreement that the field of leadership ethics needs to be explored and clarified.[2] One of the challenges in understanding ethical leadership is that it not only needs to be interpreted globally but also at a high enough level of complexity to guide us in meeting ethical challenges and making good choices. In his 2012 article "Paying More Than Lip Service to Business Ethics," Doug Guthrie, dean of the George Washington University School of Business, says, "The lesson of the last decade is that when ethics fails to temper economic passions we all suffer, from the individual to the corporation to the society."[3]

It is relatively easy to make decisions using just one ethical leadership lens. This greatly simplifies decision making. But thinking in only one dimension of ethical leadership puts us at great risk for unethical choices and behavior. Even ethical leadership "experts" can get stuck, missing important aspects of what it means to lead ethically. Here are some examples of what can happen when we become too focused on one aspect of ethical leadership to the exclusion of the others:

- **Putting people first (but ignoring the environment):** A business earns a national award for its people practices while polluting the stream near its manufacturing plant.
- **Focusing on ethical scholarship (but ignoring interpersonal behavior):** An ethical leadership author uses judging and blaming language while trying to educate others about responsible leadership choices.
- **Using ethical branding (but choosing suppliers who don't use fair labor practices):** A company is transparent and responsible in its choices of ingredients, taking care to protect customers. That same company has failed to check the ethics of every link

in its supply chain and is unintentionally supporting fair trade violations.

Openness to Learning

He who knows only his own side of the case knows little of that.

—John Stuart Mill

On the journey to ethical leadership, certain mindsets prepare us better than others. Because we lead in the midst of constant change, one of the most important factors that ethical leadership requires is openness to learning. Without it, we can become stuck in our own "rightness," believing that we understand how to lead and that our views are the right ones.

When we start believing that we know all there is to know, it is easy to become judgmental about views different from our own. In the meantime, the world continues to change and our position becomes more and more outdated. Failing to adapt to change, we may make decisions that result in serious unintended consequences.

By contrast, the learner's approach to ethical leadership requires us to be intentionally open to opinions that differ from ours. Mark Gerzon, in his book *Leading Through Conflict*, shares Jeanette Gerzon's description of the optimal level of openness: "The challenge is for each of us to find a place in ourselves from which to listen, a place so grounded that we can listen even if it might change our beliefs."[4]

Thinking Beyond Ourselves

Our task must be to free ourselves by widening our circle of compassion to embrace all living creatures and the whole of nature and its beauty.

—Albert Einstein

In the quest for ethical leadership, it is easy to get caught up in the words. Dozens of different terms are used to describe different types and branches of ethics. For example, there's meta-ethics, normative ethics, descriptive ethics, applied ethics, business ethics, role ethics, principle-based ethics, character ethics, virtue ethics, value ethics, relational ethics, social ethics, environmental ethics, deontology, consequentialism, and utilitarianism. Underlying all of these terms is the need to think beyond ourselves.

Ethics in leadership is about how we think, behave, and perform our work. It's about how we make decisions and how we hold ourselves accountable for thinking beyond our own interests. It should not be watered down to a detached philosophical debate. If you've watched the news lately, you know how much we need clear guidance that helps us think beyond ourselves in all of the scope and complexity that "beyond ourselves" represents.

In Chapter Two, in the interests of getting "beyond ourselves," I explore how ethical leadership brings out the best in people and organizations and how doing that offers a clear business advantage.

2

A Business Advantage

New studies, surveys and empirical evidence from companies reveal that stock prices are higher, costs are lower and employees more satisfied at companies with reputations for ethical business practices and good governance.

—LRN

Ethical leadership not only helps build people-friendly groups, organizations, and communities but also offers clear business advantages. Consistent ethical leadership contributes to key business metrics, makes work more meaningful, and brings out the best in people and organizations.

Business Metrics
Ethical leadership increases organizational competitiveness and makes businesses great places to work. By creating a compelling climate and proactively using responsible business practices, ethical leadership positively

impacts a number of important business metrics. These metrics benefit organizational profitability, customers, employees, and communities. Here are some of the metrics that consistent ethical leadership improves:

Business Metric:	Source:
• Profitability	Ethics Resource Center[5]
• Customer retention	Edelman Trust Barometer[6]
• Employee satisfaction	Ethics Resource Center[7]
• Productivity	Josephson Institute[8]
• Employee engagement	Ethics Resource Center[9]
• Customer attraction	Edelman Trust Barometer[10]
• Risk	LRN[11]
• Employee retention	Ethics and Compliance Officer Association and Ethics Resource Center[12]

The kind of ethical leadership that offers business advantages is sincere and intentional. It is transparent, free from pretense or falsehood, and service oriented. Companies that use pseudo-ethical practices to try to gain these business advantages will be disappointed. Consumers, employees, and the marketplace are increasingly able to spot deceptive practices like spin (pretending you're more ethical than you really are by twisting statistics and words), "greenwashing" (pretending to be more environmentally responsible than you really are), fake endorsements, and fibs. In an increasingly responsibility-aware marketplace, these practices are not rewarded.

Organizational Transformation

When leaders use sincere ethical leadership, they transform their organizations in positive ways. I have been asked by leaders, "What do you do if you are in a company that is not making it a priority to lead ethically, but you know that it's the right thing to do?"

It is very difficult to lead in a setting in which your personal goals conflict with or don't align well with the organization's goals. If there are serious issues that you believe place you at risk by being in this setting, you may have to leave. If not, and assuming you want to stay, my advice is to lead from where you are, setting a positive example for the rest of the organization. One leader *can* begin to change an organizational culture. When other leaders see dozens of qualified internal applicants applying for your open positions, senior management raving about your department's productivity, and your team having fun getting it all done, they'll want to know your secret.

Why does ethical leadership transform organizations? Quite simply, it is the kind of leadership that brings out the very best in people. By bringing out the best in people, we release a great deal of potential energy that can be used to forward the mission. Bringing out the best in people and organizations also attracts customers, employees, and partners, opening up opportunities for growth. By proactively preventing ethical leadership problems, businesses can also compete better in tight markets when other organizations may be diverting resources to solve ethical problems.

Meaningful Work and Organizational Potential

People enjoy working when they are valued and treated with respect. Customers enjoy buying from companies that have happy employees who care about customers. Because of these and other factors, companies that consistently strive to do business ethically tend to outperform their counterparts that don't make ethical leadership a priority.

Successful ethical leaders improve lives and communities and make a difference in the world. For a growing number of people seeking meaning in their lives and work, ethical leadership meets an important need.

Intentional ethical leadership builds trust and credibility. It creates a high-trust workplace where people are free to bring their ideas and enthusiasm to work. Creating that type of culture releases untapped potential in your people and your organization.

To imagine the improvements that ethical leadership could make in your organization, ask yourself these questions:

1. How much more potential does our organization have that ethical leadership could bring out?
2. How engaged are employees in their work, and how could ethical leadership increase their engagement?

11

3. What business metrics could be improved through ethical leadership?
4. What one or two areas of leadership have the most potential for improvement?
5. How could ethical leadership make a difference in these areas?

Many people proactively eat healthy foods, take vitamins, and exercise to stay well. An investment in ethical leadership is a similar investment in organizational wellness and long-term business success. You will find information about recent reports that make the business case for ethical leadership in the endnotes that conclude this book.

Now that we have explored some of the business advantages of ethical leadership, let's move on to defining the kinds of responsibilities that are part of ethical leadership. In Chapter Three, I define the 7 Lenses of Ethical Responsibility. Each lens represents a different perspective, and these different perspectives help explain why people sometimes disagree so bitterly over "the right thing" to do.

3

7 Lenses of Ethical Responsibility

Creativity is a lot like looking at the world through a kaleidoscope.
You look at a set of elements, the same ones everyone else sees, but then
reassemble those floating bits and pieces into an enticing new possibility.

—Rosabeth Moss Kanter

Perhaps one reason we haven't easily agreed on what ethical leadership means is that we have been looking at it through a microscope, at its individual parts. Looking at it that way doesn't help us resolve seemingly competing views or provide sufficient clarity in increasingly complex situations.

By contrast, looking at ethical leadership through a kaleidoscope lets us look at the parts across multiple dimensions. Only that broader and multidimensional view of the parts provides a perspective that is whole.

Clarity in Multiple Dimensions

When we begin to define ethical leadership through a kaleidoscope, it becomes clear that it means many things at the same time on many different levels. Ethical leadership is both multidimensional and evolving. It is an opportunity to bring out the best in people and organizations and a leadership responsibility. Because it is multidimensional and changing, using overly simple approaches such as "Do the right thing" may not direct us to what the most ethical choices would be. Unless our own individual values are broad, global, and long term, they won't easily guide us to ethical decisions in a global economy.

It isn't surprising that ethical leadership is inherently multidimensional. It is an interdisciplinary topic at the intersection of a collection of fields of study that are usually discussed separately. These include leadership, human growth and development, moral development, applied business ethics, learning and performance improvement, psychology, systems thinking, sustainability, corporate social responsibility, global business, and the list goes on.

Not only is ethical leadership multidimensional and interdisciplinary, it introduces multiple principles and various interpretations of their meaning, application, and priority. To add more complexity to the puzzle, Joanne Ciulla points out that "Philosophers who specialize in ethics see their subject differently than do social scientists."[13]

Ethical leadership is continually being redefined, as research in multiple areas provides clarity about human well-being and how to lead people responsibly in organizations. The ethical leadership of a business, through ethical products and services, adds another layer to our understanding. We not only need to lead people ethically but we must also make ethical business decisions that impact many other stakeholders.

As I explored in my March, 2010 article for *Training and Development* titled "Leadership Ethics Training: Why Is It So Hard To Get It Right?", ethical leadership moves into moral territory because it involves values, world views, and ethical principles.[14] It is part of psychology and human growth and development because it involves people, motivation and learning. It will be implemented within organizations, so it must be considered in the context of business, organizational relationships, effectiveness, and results.

To understand all these layers of ethical leadership, we need to use more than one perspective.

The 7 Lenses of Ethical Responsibility

The 7 Lenses are different ways of thinking about ethical responsibility. While the perspectives we see using the 7 Lenses are not new, seeing all seven connected aspects of ethical responsibility together may be revolutionary. When we use all seven together, we see a kaleidoscopic view of ethical leadership that honors its inherent complexity.

As you continue to read, consider which of the 7 Lenses best reflects your beliefs about ethical responsibility. Which other perspectives do you honor in your day-to-day decisions? Which ones does your deepest moral sense tell you that you should be honoring?

Understanding the 7 Lenses of Ethical Responsibility

Ethics is knowing the difference between what you have a right to do and what is right to do.

—Potter Stewart

To get a broad understanding of ethical leadership, we will look at it through each of the 7 Lenses of Ethical Responsibility. Generally speaking, the narrowest interpretation of ethical responsibility is reflected in the lenses on the left, and the broadest interpretation is reflected in the lenses on the right. We'll start at the left on the graphic on page 17 with the narrowest interpretation, the Profit Lens.

Lens One: Profit

Honoring the Bottom Line

✳ no margin, no
mission ✳

All the gold which is under or upon the earth
is not enough to give in exchange for virtue.

—Plato

We can begin to understand the 7 Lenses by clearly envisioning how profit fits into an ethical leadership framework. The key question of the Profit Lens is, "How much money will this make?"

The Profit Lens honors the ongoing money concerns of a business. Unless a business is structured in a way that removes concerns about profitability, it does need to make a profit on an ongoing basis.[15] Businesses need profits to pay employees, to make products, to grow the business, and to give back to the communities they serve.

Because profits are fundamental to business survival, this lens is one that leaders must use as they pursue their work. Without profitability, a business may struggle along, unable to pursue its mission well enough to attract new customers. Without profitability, a business may not be able to create solutions that meet real needs. Unfortunately, in our society, some leaders have promoted profitability to the level of a value and use it as the sole basis for making choices.

UNETHICAL PROFITABILITY
(MAXIMIZING PROFITS WITHOUT CONCERN FOR STAKEHOLDERS)

While profitability is important, it doesn't take the place of a moral evaluation of our choices. If it does, we're putting money where morality should be. If we use profitability as a main "value," then we may automatically exclude concern for how a given decision will impact others. Will the cheap paint we buy from a vendor with lax ethical practices contain lead or other harmful ingredients? Will the cheapest or "lowest bidder" parts in our medical equipment fail, leading to patient deaths and lawsuits?

A profit focus not balanced with business responsibility reflects a high concern for individual gain and a belief that we are not responsible

7 Lenses of Ethical Responsibility

1 Profit	2 Law	3 Character	4 People	5 Communities	6 Planet	7 Greater Good
Make Money	Comply	Be Moral	Care	Serve	Sustain	Do Good
Important but has no inherent moral grounding --- If this lens is used alone, money is where morality should be	Grounded in the punishment threshold --- Focus is on avoiding penalties by complying with laws and regulations, not on honoring principles	Grounded in integrity and moral values --- Thoughts, words, and deeds are aligned, setting an example for others	Grounded in concern for people --- Focus is on respecting all others, respecting differences, caring about people, and avoiding harm	Grounded in concern for communities --- Focus is on helping those in need, building strong communities, and serving others and society	Grounded in concern for the planet --- Focus is on respecting life and nature, conserving natural resources, and doing business sustainably	Grounded in concern for the long-term greater good --- Focus is on benefiting society and future generations in order to make the world better

to our constituents—our customers, our employees, our communities, and our environment. Economics is one way of thinking about profit, but there are additional perspectives that give us the full picture.

Using only an economic view of profit and no guiding values when making decisions means that we ignore the risks in our industry and the needs and expectations of our customers. We ignore the complexity that is inherent in running a company and balancing customer needs and wants with employee engagement, product safety, environmental and societal impact, and many other connected variables. Ignoring these variables increases the chances that we will stumble (either knowingly or not) into ethical violations. The Profit Lens is important, but since it has no inherent moral grounding, it cannot be used alone.

Ethical Profitability (Profiting Responsibly)

In ethical leadership, the quest for profits is tempered with concern for the welfare of those we serve. The moral leader knows that business is not win-lose; we can meet the needs of multiple stakeholders *and* achieve our goals profitably. While we do have a business obligation to keep our businesses profitable, the quest for profit must be balanced with ethical responsibility as represented by the other six lenses.

When we are focused on ethical profitability, we ask questions like, "How can we ensure product safety and still make a profit?" and "How will we monitor our supply chain to be sure all of our suppliers demonstrate ethical practices?" Here, profit takes its place as part of a bigger system of responsibility and value creation.

As James Rouse said, "Profit is a reward for important service well-rendered, and not the legitimate purpose of business in its own right."[16] This way of thinking about profit incorporates a service mindset and a broad understanding of business leadership responsibilities. Michael Porter and Mark Kramer of Harvard University, in their article "Creating Shared Value," describe shared value as profit done the right way:

> *The solution lies in the principle of shared value, which involves creating economic value in a way that also creates value for*

society by addressing its needs and challenges. Businesses must
reconnect company success with social progress. [17]

When we connect our economic success with the success of others and society, we are fulfilling the responsibility of leadership in a way that simultaneously improves society and our bottom line.

We do focus on profit, but at a higher level that also includes our corresponding responsibilities. When we honor all 7 Lenses, we carefully balance our profits with our broader impact on multiple stakeholders. In an ethical leadership context, then, the Profit Lens looks at profiting responsibly.

Lens Two: Law
Honoring the Punishment Threshold

> *It is not desirable to cultivate a respect*
> *for the law, so much as for the right.*
>
> —Henry David Thoreau

In addition to profiting responsibly, ethical leaders follow laws and regulations. Aristotle observed that "At his best, man is the noblest of all animals; separated from law and justice he is the worst."[18]

The key question of the Law Lens is, "How can we avoid punishment and penalties?" Some people think that honoring laws is what ethical leadership is all about, but laws actually represent the minimum standard in a society. Below this level, people are punished and businesses are penalized for their actions. If we aim at the level of following laws and regulations in order to stay out of jail and avoid fines, we are aiming too low. Laws are boundaries used to guide our behavior away from behaviors that may harm others or infringe on their rights and freedoms.

Profit or Power-Based Approach to Law

A leader honoring the Law Lens could still make decisions for self gain without concern for what that gain does to other constituents. For example, if I understand ethical responsibility only through a Law Lens, I may be honoring laws but only to avoid punishment. I may also work legal angles to my own advantage, looking for loopholes to maximize personal or organizational gain. Imagine a company boardroom in which lawyers and senior managers discuss recent cases of bullying in their industry using a power-based approach to law. In this scenario, their focus will be on identifying the legal connections they each have that could be "worked" if they ever have a violation instead of working together to ensure that all employees are treated with respect.

VALUES-BASED APPROACH TO LAW

To fully honor ethical leadership, we need to reach far beyond the punishment threshold that laws represent. When we do that, we accept full responsibility for our choices and actively work to avoid harm. Imagine a company boardroom in which leaders discuss recent cases of bullying in their industry using a values-based approach to law. In this scenario, they proactively review the expectations and performance management systems that make it clear that respectful interpersonal behavior is the minimum standard in their organization.

Using a values-based approach to the law gives us ethical grounding. We obey the law but do not see honoring that law as our ultimate goal. Using this mindset, we honor laws as the minimum boundaries but also aim much higher to make choices that honor our broader ethical responsibilities.

Lens Three: Character
Honoring Personal Ethics

> *When we see persons of worth, we should think of equaling them; when we see persons of a contrary character, we should turn inwards and examine ourselves.*
>
> —Confucius

In addition to profiting responsibly and honoring laws, ethical leaders demonstrate character and a high level of personal congruence. They take great care to ensure that their thoughts, words, and deeds are aligned, and they are willing to do what they ask of others.

The key question of the Character Lens is, "How can I demonstrate integrity, congruence, and moral awareness?" Leaders honoring the Character Lens demonstrate honesty, integrity, and trustworthiness. They are morally aware and stay competent as the world changes. Such leaders wrestle with decisions and consider which solution best supports the company policy, individual integrity, and group trust. Using this lens, we consider how well we:

- Demonstrate congruence in our thoughts, words, and deeds
- Demonstrate moral awareness
- Stay competent as the world changes, and
- Practice what we ask of others

Some leaders believe that if we have "good character," we will always know the right thing to do. I believe that while integrity, personal congruence, and moral awareness are important, they represent only personal ethics. Ethical leadership also requires considering our responsibility more broadly to include interpersonal, societal, and environmental ethics. Having good character can help us lead ethically in all of the other dimensions, but it doesn't work in isolation. We also have to demonstrate ethical leadership through our words and actions.

Lens Four: People
Honoring Interpersonal Ethics

Educating the mind without educating the heart is no education at all.

—Aristotle

In addition to profiting responsibly, following laws, and demonstrating good character, ethical leaders respect and care for others. The key question of the People Lens is, "How can I respect and care for people?"

Honoring the People Lens is a respectful way of approaching business that sees building positive relationships as a critical part of business leadership. Key questions to consider using this lens include:

- How will this option benefit or harm people?
- How will it impact morale?
- How will it affect employee well-being and satisfaction?
- How will it affect customers and partners?

Using the People Lens, we know that our business success depends on our ability to engage the people we employ and the people we serve in meaningful ways. We will want to support programs that have a positive effect on people, even if there are other choices that are legal and highly profitable. Honoring this lens also means respecting others and using positive interpersonal behavior. We consider our impact on others broadly, both in terms of positive leadership support and avoiding harm. We carefully consider the long-term success and well-being of people.

Lens Five: Communities
Honoring Societal Ethics

The Greek philosophers have also contributed the notion that life in community is a good in itself and our actions should contribute to that life.

—Markkula Center for Applied Ethics, Santa Clara University

In addition to profiting responsibly, following laws, demonstrating good character, and respecting and caring for people, ethical leaders also honor and serve communities. The key question of the Communities Lens is, "How can we serve communities?"

A concern for communities may include the availability of important shared services such as housing, education, transportation, clean water, social systems, parks, and libraries. Supporting these kinds of collective community resources helps make life better for everyone who lives there and makes the community appealing as a place to live and work.

Questions to consider using this lens include:

- How can we improve the communities we serve?
- What unmet needs are there that we are able to meet?
- How could we engage our employees and partners in helping meet those needs?

Ethical leaders realize that they are an integral part of communities and that their success is dependent on the health and welfare of those communities. Participating in community service not only benefits the community but also engages employees in meaningful ways. Businesses contribute to communities in ways that include volunteerism, philanthropy, and program sponsorships that help meet otherwise unmet community needs. Some businesses are becoming active partners with communities to accomplish positive change that neither could accomplish alone.

Lens Six: Planet
Honoring Life and Ecosystems

For the sake of our health, our children and grandchildren and even our economic well-being, we must make protecting the planet our top priority.

—David Suzuki

We have explored how ethical leaders profit responsibly, follow laws, demonstrate good character, respect and care for people, and contribute to communities in positive ways. Ethical leaders also consider their impact on life, ecosystems, and the planet. The key question of the Planet Lens is, "How can we honor life and ecosystems?"

Considering our impact on the natural resources and living systems of our planet reflects an understanding that we are part of nature and reliant on it for our survival. It reflects a responsibility to preserve the natural world and its resources for the future. Leaders honoring the Planet Lens believe that we should not pollute or damage our environment or the natural life that depends on it.

Businesses using this lens use systems thinking to understand the connectedness of business systems with natural systems and communities.

They may be working on ways to reach a zero footprint, or no negative impact on the environment.

Questions to ask using this lens include:

- What is our net effect on the environment and what will be the long-term impact over hundreds of years?
- How can we improve our use of recycled and reclaimed materials and reduce our use of new resources?
- What are others in our industry doing to reduce environmental impact while still making a profit?"

A leader honoring the Planet Lens will want to support programs and policies that do not harm the planet and will want to preserve natural resources for future generations.

Lens Seven: Greater Good
Honoring Future Generations

. . . an underlying moral presence shared by all humanity—a set of precepts so fundamental that they dissolve borders, transcend races, and outlast cultural traditions.

—Dr. Rushworth Kidder

In addition to honoring all six of the other lenses of ethical responsibility, ethical businesses that embrace responsibility for the greater good find new ways to add value for future generations. This leadership is greater than ourselves, greater than our own interests, greater than our own works, and greater than our own lifetimes. This is the kind of leadership that leaves a positive legacy that many future generations will enjoy. The key question of the Greater Good Lens is, "How can we make the world better for future generations?"

At this level of thinking, business leaders use collaboration and co-creation to solve difficult problems that cross boundaries at the levels of company, community, and society. They look at forecasts and trends, think of the business world as a global community, and work toward a successful future for that global community. Using this lens, we evaluate our decisions in terms of their positive impact on the collective well-being of future generations. This includes future generations in other countries, people of other political parties, people in other industries, and people whom we may never meet.

Making decisions that consider the greater good includes thinking about:

- The impact on people and their quality of life many generations into the future
- The positive benefits this choice provides for our communities, society at large, and the world, and
- The global impact if everyone did what we are planning to do

The Greater Good Lens is the broadest, the longest term, and the most responsible of the 7 Lenses. Companies using this level of thinking to determine their actions on a daily basis are true global citizens. Policies and programs they put into place now will enhance the quality of life for future generations. Those policies and programs will honor economic, human, ecological, and societal goals. The greater good reflects a level of global service, inclusion, respect, and care that results in a better world for all.

I am seeing a movement toward leadership for the greater good as the expected level of ethics in a global society. Consumers are evaluating companies on their ethics when they purchase, and an increasing number of them are thinking inclusively and long term. Leaders who do not embrace the greater good will miss opportunities to reach ethically-aware consumers and to enhance lives and communities.

Using All 7 Lenses

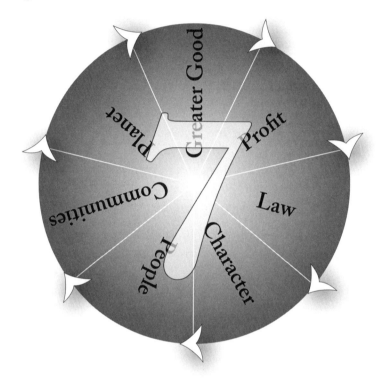

Using a multi-lens understanding of ethical responsibility in organizations helps us understand why it is so hard for people to agree on policies and programs that impact our societies. It helps us understand what we need to change. Profit alone does not work as a lens of ethical responsibility because it has no inherent moral grounding. The Law Lens alone does not work because it aims too low, at the punishment threshold. The People Lens alone does not work because it does not necessarily include making a profit, following the law, demonstrating character, or honoring communities, the environment, or society's future. And so on. Each lens is part of ethical leadership, and when any one is ignored, we fail to lead ethically in its fullest interpretation.

We are part of a shared economy, with shared resources and shared social channels of communication. In a global economy, individual leadership choices have a magnified impact on others around the world. That impact may either be positive or negative depending on our choices. As we learn more about what all of this means, both the ideal of ethical leadership and the minimum standards for ethical leadership are being raised. The higher standards reflect an understanding of our magnified impact on others in a connected society with limited resources.

While the 7 Lenses have been discussed here individually, they actually represent an expanding continuum of views on ethical responsibility, from narrow (profit) to broad (greater good).

7 Compounding Lenses

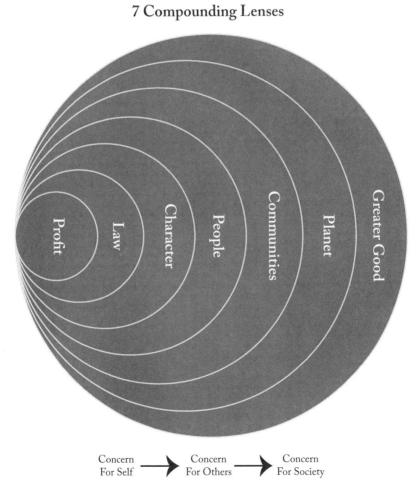

Starting with the Profit Lens (concern for self), each lens we add to our perspective gives us a new sense of clarity about what ethical responsibility means. Each lens we add has a compounding effect that takes our leadership to a higher level. It is no accident that this movement from the narrowest to the broadest lens parallels the movement from concern for only self to concern for self and others that is reflected in Maslow's hierarchy of needs, and further development toward self and society that is reflected in Kohlberg's stages of moral development, Erik Erikson's theory of psychosocial development, and other human development models.

While leaders sometimes argue intensely over which choices are "right," a more productive approach would be to discuss which ones honor the most and the highest lenses. Each of the 7 Lenses gives us part of the full picture. Only by using all seven in daily leadership do we fully balance our interests with our responsibilities.

I said earlier that each lens we add takes our leadership to a higher level as we incorporate more lenses into our view of ethical responsibility. As we learn, we move from concern for self, to concern for self and others, to concern for self, others and society. The ultimate goal is to incorporate all 7 Lenses into daily leadership and to demonstrate the highest level of responsibility.

The beauty of this journey is that we start from wherever we are and work toward our destination. Starting with the Profit Lens, take a moment to reflect on which lenses you have already incorporated into your view of ethical responsibility, and consider which lenses represent where you would like to be. For example, if you already honor the Profit, Law and Character Lenses in your daily leadership, your development goal could be to look for ways to actively demonstrate concern for people and communities.

When we are open to learning, and when we explore ethical leadership in all its complexity, it becomes clear that we need to consider our impact broadly. This means adding additional lenses to our decision-making process until we are using them all. Here are some examples of what that broad view using all 7 Lenses looks like in action:

- Considering our impact on others and society
- Thinking beyond short-term gain to long-term impact
- Thinking beyond personal values to global values
- Thinking beyond profit to contributions to society
- Anticipating and preventing unintended consequences of our actions
- Considering the impact of our business on the environment
- Improving lives and communities
- Making a difference in the world

Using all 7 Lenses together offers us a multidimensional view of ethical leadership. This view helps us honor our responsibilities broadly and act as model global citizens. How can we incorporate this multidimensional view into our daily leadership? In Part Two of this book, I introduce 14 Guiding Principles that honor all of the 7 Lenses of Ethical Responsibility.

Part 2

14 Guiding Principles That Honor All 7 Lenses in Daily Leadership

We now have 7 Lenses through which to understand ethical leadership, but how do we incorporate these 7 Lenses into our day-to-day decisions and actions?

If we use only our own personal values in defining our understanding of ethical leadership through each lens, we each might be using a different definition of what is "right." To get past that problem, we need instead to apply some universal values, some underlying moral concepts that most people would agree are important.[19] This provides a context for leadership ethics that can be discussed in leadership development programs and classrooms. Further, it allows us to stop talking about who's right and start talking about which choices are most ethically right.

The 14 Guiding Principles this book proposes help us honor all 7 Lenses of Ethical Responsibility. These principles are based on a blend of the standards for responsible business, emerging global values, and the wisdom of classical and modern ethicists. They include not only a leader's personal congruence but also a leader's behavior in interactions with others and the world. Ethicists and notable leaders from different fields, countries, and times have championed these principles. When they are followed, they help us build better organizations and a better world.

It is easy to embrace one or two of the 7 Lenses and mistakenly think that we understand the whole. These 14 Guiding Principles are suggested as a guide for how to honor all 7 Lenses in daily leadership. In developing this list, I began with simple and widely accepted ethical and moral principles, including:

- Do good without doing harm
- Be honest
- Be fair
- Recognize and respect others' rights
- Behave with autonomy and respect autonomy in others
- Exhibit personal integrity (e.g., live up to your word)

After considering the complexity of organizational life, I then developed the longer list of ethically-relevant leadership behaviors introduced below and discussed in the next four chapters. These 14 Guiding Principles are not separate. Each connects with and supports the other principles in such a way that missing any one of them could lead to an ethical lapse. Together, these fourteen principles represent the kind of ethical leadership that will bring out the best in people, organizations, and communities, and they are broad enough to provide a framework for leading ethically in any context.

14 Guiding Principles of Ethical Leadership
Lead With a Moral Compass
Principle 1: Demonstrate Personal Congruence
Principle 2: Be Morally Aware
Principle 3: Stay Competent
Principle 4: Model Expected Performance and Leadership

Lead in Ways That Bring Out the Best in Others
Principle 5: Respect Others
Principle 6: Respect Boundaries
Principle 7: Trust and Be Trustworthy
Principle 8: Communicate Openly
Principle 9: Generate Effective and Ethical Performance

Lead With Positive Intent and Impact
Principle 10: Think Like an Ethical Leader
Principle 11: Do Good Without Doing Harm
Principle 12: Work for Mutually Beneficial Solutions

Lead for the Greater Good
Principle 13: Protect Our Planet for Future Generations
Principle 14: Improve Our Global Society for Future Generations

In the following four chapters, in light of these 14 Guiding Principles, I explore how to honor all 7 Lenses in daily leadership. As you read these chapters, please ponder a recent difficult decision or decisions you had to make. How well did your decision-making process incorporate all 14 Guiding Principles? If it didn't include all fourteen, how could you have honored more principles without sacrificing your goals?

4

Lead With a Moral Compass

Two things fill the mind with ever new and increasing admiration and awe, the more often and steadily we reflect upon them: the starry heavens above me and the moral law within me.

—Immanuel Kant

14 Guiding Principles of Ethical Leadership

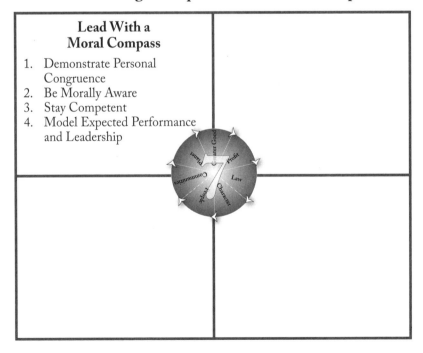

Lead With a Moral Compass	
1. Demonstrate Personal Congruence 2. Be Morally Aware 3. Stay Competent 4. Model Expected Performance and Leadership	

P hilosophers and leaders from a variety of disciplines have described what they call a moral compass, a powerful inner sense of right and wrong that guides our moral choices. This powerful sense of right and wrong is grounded in moral awareness and a sensitivity to how we impact others. In this chapter, I describe four guiding principles that combine to serve as our moral compass. These four aspects of ethical leadership help us build ethical workplaces, lead others in ethical ways, and lead well in a global context.

The Scope of the First Four Guiding Principles

Principle One: Demonstrate Personal Congruence and Principle Two: Be Morally Aware reflect inner qualities. These are sometimes included in the list of personal qualities necessary for "good moral character" and are necessary for effective and ethical leadership.

Some would suggest that "character" develops early in life and that it is impossible to improve moral character in adulthood. As this thinking goes, either you have it or you don't, and if you don't, it's too late now.

To some extent, that may be true, which is why it is important to screen potential employees for qualities beyond technical competence and to hire those who demonstrate honesty, integrity, and trustworthiness. However, I do believe that moral qualities *can* be fostered, nurtured, and enhanced throughout life, and that the work environment can support their continued development.

Principle Three: Stay Competent and Principle Four: Model Expected Performance and Leadership overlap in an important way. Behaving in the ways we expect others to behave needs to include modeling the level of ethical competence we expect. Using the four principles that help us Lead With a Moral Compass can be helpful in the process of learning to respect ourselves as leaders. When we respect ourselves, we may be more likely to act respectfully toward others.

Principle One: Demonstrate Personal Congruence

Be as you wish to seem.

—Socrates

Personal congruence has been variously defined as:

- having all parts of one's body and mind in harmony[20]
- achieving rapport within oneself; the absence of major internal inconsistencies
- being at peace within yourself, not at war with yourself
- demonstrating consistency about who you *are* (values and beliefs), what you *feel*, what you *say*, and what you *do*; more deeply, your desires (intentions), your thoughts (attention), your feelings, and your actions are aligned with your core values[21]

The person who demonstrates personal congruence is likely to be perceived by others as sincere, stable, centered, consistent, and well grounded. If you are this person, your integrity can be trusted and your behavior is reasonably predictable. You say what you mean, you mean what you say, and you practice what you preach.

Stephen M. R. Covey, author of *The Speed of Trust*, writes that "People who are congruent act in harmony with their deepest values and beliefs . . . The voice they listen and respond to is the quiet voice of conscience."[22]

In addition to being personally congruent, ethical leaders are also contextually congruent. They apply the same high ethical standards in all of their many roles. As Dr. Rushworth Kidder said, "There is no dividing up ethics into the compartments of private ethics and public ethics. There's only ethics."[23]

Leaders who demonstrate congruence have all of their roles, their internal beliefs, and their external behaviors aligned so closely that there is no difference between them. What they say and do at work reliably matches the way they act on weekends. Their words express their true thoughts, and those thoughts are grounded in a deep sense of personal values.

PRINCIPLE ONE CASE STUDY:
LEADING WITH CONGRUENCE

John is a middle-aged retail executive who has not had much formal leadership training but is well respected by the members of his team. His judgments are thoughtful and consistent, he is open to suggestions and ideas, and his interactions are clear, respectful, and encouraging, even when someone has fallen short of meeting goals. He maintains very high standards and readily helps his team members develop. They know what to expect from him, and they have learned they can count on him if they need advice or support. His division has always been one of the most cooperative and productive teams in the company.

Sharon is a new manager in the same company, fresh from an MBA program at a prestigious university. She brings a great deal of confidence and many new and innovative ideas to her work. In her first week on the job, she implements new policies and sets higher performance goals for each team member. Within her first three months, she revises those policies and changes the goals several times without explaining her reasons for the changes. She spends a lot of time in her office on the computer or telephone rather than on the floor with her team, and she tends to arrive late and leave early. Sharon is perceived as inconsistent and unpredictable, sometimes praising good work and sometimes ignoring it while pushing for even better performance. Sometimes she is in a very pleasant mood; at other times she is quick to express impatience or have angry outbursts. Her team members tend to avoid her when they can, and they have begun to ease their tension by placing bets on the "mood of the day." Her team has become the least productive in the company, and there are three requests for transfers to other departments on her desk.

OBSERVATIONS ON THE CASE

In this example, John demonstrates personal congruence while Sharon does not. John's team is experiencing high levels of trust, loyalty, and performance, while Sharon's team is experiencing high levels of frustration and turnover.

Because we ask a lot from those we lead, we need to be sure that they can count on us to use consistent and congruent behavior, to model expected performance, and to support their individual and collective success.

What Personally Congruent Leaders Do

Personally congruent leaders are consistent in their feelings, thoughts, words, and actions, which helps them create high-trust workplaces. In addition, personally congruent leaders:

- Are sincere, stable, centered, and well grounded
- Have a strong conscience and listen to it
- Make thoughtful decisions
- Act in alignment with their deepest values
- Say what they mean and mean what they say
- Practice what they ask others to do
- Can be counted on by employees and colleagues
- Are consistent in their thoughts, words, and actions

Principle Two: Be Morally Aware

What the statesman is most anxious to produce is a certain moral character in his fellow citizens, namely a disposition to virtue and the performance of virtuous actions.

—Aristotle

Leaders who are morally aware notice things that have moral or ethical implications, whether that involves their behavior, others' actions, or broader organizational policies. Below are a few examples of how morally aware leaders behave, with questions for reflection. As you read, think about how well you demonstrate moral awareness in your own leadership.

Morally aware leaders:

1. **Notice any unintended consequences of their actions.**
   Questions for reflection: Have I instituted a new policy in order to try to streamline or improve work? Did I notice whether or not it had the intended effect? Am I certain it did not inadvertently harm someone or create conflict within the team?
2. **Respect rules and laws.**
   Questions for reflection: Am I clear about the general laws and policies that apply to everyone in my agency or organization, including its leaders? Am I attending to whether I follow those rules and laws myself, rather than treating my own behavior as an exception to the rule? If these are good rules, why don't they also apply to me?
3. **Notice rules or laws that seem unreasonable, unfair, or harmful.**
   Respecting rules and laws does not imply that one should blindly obey bad ones. Questions for reflection: Do I notice organizational rules that should be changed and then participate in changing them rather than simply ignoring them?
4. **Honor their obligations.**
   Questions for reflection: Do I think carefully before making promises or commitments or do I sometimes make promises I am unlikely to be able to keep? When I find that I am unable to meet an obligation, do I notice the problem and deal with it directly with anyone who might be affected?
5. **Notice potential conflicts of interest in order to avoid them when possible.**
   Conflicts of interest are circumstances in which one relationship or obligation conflicts with another in a way that would affect objectivity. Questions for reflection: Do I anticipate potential conflicts of interest and avoid them when possible? If they are unavoidable, do I notice them when they happen and address them with the parties involved? Do I need to test my objectivity by consulting with a mentor or leader?

6. **Balance competing interests.**

   In contrast to conflicts of interest, *competing* interests are unavoidable, and negotiating them is an ongoing responsibility for any leader. Questions for reflection: Do I notice when competing interests are present, acknowledge them, and decide how to balance them in a way that gives priority to the values considered most important in my organization? Do I use a structured decision-making process that helps me make such determinations?

7. **Avoid participating in corruption, bribery, extortion, and the like; also notice them in others and do not condone them.**

   It is not possible to avoid corruption, bribery, and extortion unless I am first willing to notice them and identify them as such, describe them to myself for what they really are, and recognize why they are morally wrong (not just legally wrong) and harmful. Questions for reflection: Do I always notice such practices, or do I (and/or my organization) have a "blind spot" about them?

8. **Take responsibility for their decisions, behavior, and actions.**

   Morally aware leaders take responsibility for the impact of their decisions, behavior, and actions. Questions for reflection: Do I take responsibility for my choices, avoiding blame and defensiveness?

PRINCIPLE TWO CASE STUDY: NOT MORALLY AWARE

Chris has just been hired to be in charge of a new project at a publishing house where honesty, integrity, and trustworthiness have always been key values. She previously played a similar role in another publishing company that had a very different corporate culture.

It has come to the attention of Chris's superiors that she has signed a large supply contract with a vendor who sells inferior products at high prices but who has provided her with free trips. In addition, Chris allows some of her employees to charge personal items on their company credit cards. Finally, although the company has a clear policy about how vacation time is to be fairly earned and calculated, Chris has made promises of extra

continues ▶

vacation time to some but not all of her employees while asking them in return to do personal favors for her.

OBSERVATIONS ON THE CASE

Chris's decision to accept valuable trips from a vendor with whom she has a contractual relationship shows that she is not morally aware. Accepting the trips is a conflict of interest. Ignoring the conflict of interest makes it easier for her to focus on the advantages (to her) of choosing this company as a key vendor even though the products are inferior. Her decision to grant extra vacation time to some employees who handle her personal business and to allow employees to charge personal items on their company credit cards compounds the ethical problems in this case.

In the long run, choosing to use an "inferior products at high prices" vendor will also lead to problems for the publishing house as customers become upset about the decline in quality and take their business elsewhere. Chris's self-interested choice will tarnish the reputation the company has built over many years and will soon impact its profits.

What Morally Aware Leaders Do

Morally aware leaders continually consider the ethical implications of their actions and decisions. They guard their own ethics and the ethics of their organizations carefully, and they intentionally:

- Meet their obligations
- Consider and avoid unintended consequences of their actions and decisions
- Respect laws, policies, and guidelines
- Champion changes that will help build an ethical culture in the organization
- Recognize and avoid conflicts of interest
- Balance competing interests with ethical choices
- Avoid and prevent corruption, bribery, and extortion
- Take responsibility for their decisions, behaviors, and actions

Principle Three: Stay Competent

Excellence is an art won by training and habituation.
We do not act rightly because we have virtue or excellence,
but we rather have those because we have acted rightly.
We are what we repeatedly do.
Excellence, then, is not an act but a habit.

—Aristotle

Ethical leaders conscientiously follow business trends and develop the new skills they need in an ever-changing business environment. Why is leader competence included in a book about ethical leadership? As leaders, we are paid to accomplish the organization's business goals through people. We are expected to get the job done. Getting the job done requires a wide variety of skills and abilities, depending on the industry, but the leadership skills that produce the best results evolve fairly consistently across industries. Our individual fields will also advance rapidly. It is clear that the kind of leadership and industry approaches that worked ten years ago will not be as effective in today's business world.

Let's think about what might happen to two small business owners who approach competence in different ways. When the economy hits a rough spot, one uses the time to sharpen skills and prepare for better days, learning emerging industry best practices. The other "doesn't have time to learn" and keeps doing business the same way, putting in more hours without much more reward. When the economy improves, which one will be better positioned to take advantage of the improvement and gain new clients? The one who has sharpened skills. Which one is at risk of using outdated practices and losing to competitors who are better prepared? The one who simply worked harder and didn't take time to learn and improve.

In addition to business implications, staying competent also has ethical implications. What kinds of competence do we need to manage? Multiple kinds of competence are critical for success in honoring the 14 Guiding Principles in daily leadership:

- Personal competence includes skills in self-management, thinking, organization, and time management (in turn, these support principles four and nine)
- Work and industry competence include keeping up with trends and forecasts as well as customer needs and company performance (in turn, these support principle four and provide the foundation for principles ten through fourteen)
- Interpersonal competence includes skills in working with others (these support principles five through eight)
- Intercultural and global competence provide a broad foundation for honoring the other principles
- Ethical competence (which this book is designed to help build) supports success in applying all 14 Guiding Principles

The 14 Guiding Principles

Lead With a Moral Compass
Principle 1: Demonstrate Personal Congruence
Principle 2: Be Morally Aware
Principle 3: Stay Competent
Principle 4: Model Expected Performance and Leadership

Lead in Ways That Bring Out the Best in Others
Principle 5: Respect Others
Principle 6: Respect Boundaries
Principle 7: Trust and Be Trustworthy
Principle 8: Communicate Openly
Principle 9: Generate Effective and Ethical Performance

Lead With Positive Intent and Impact
Principle 10: Think Like an Ethical Leader
Principle 11: Do Good Without Doing Harm
Principle 12: Work for Mutually Beneficial Solutions

Lead for the Greater Good
Principle 13: Protect Our Planet for Future Generations

Principle 14: Improve Our Global Society for Future Generations

Leaders who fail to stay competent are not likely to accomplish the results they seek. Worse, they are at risk of making unethical choices. Think about what will happen to the business in the following example if the leader does not quickly become competent.

PRINCIPLE THREE CASE STUDY: FAILURE TO ADAPT

Ron is a bakery owner facing hard times. Over the last two years, he's been struggling to keep his business open. If he doesn't make a profit soon, he may have to close. A new client recently approached Ron asking him to regularly supply a large quantity of gluten-free bread. He is delighted to have the business. In order to meet this demand, he will need a second supplier for rice flour, one of the main ingredients in the recipe.

Ron has been absorbed with the process of surviving the economic downturn and has not paid attention to trends in the food industry. He is unaware of the article about arsenic in rice in a recent issue of a well-known consumer magazine. When he chooses a supplier, he picks the one with the lowest prices so that he can get back to profitability more quickly. Unfortunately, he has chosen one that doesn't test its rice for arsenic. Customers who have read this recent consumer article begin calling to ask about Ron's suppliers and whether or not his product has been tested to make sure it does not contain unsafe levels of arsenic.

OBSERVATIONS ON THE CASE

Ron's brand could be on its way to becoming known as a toxic one. If the rice flour he chose does contain unsafe levels of arsenic, and if the word gets out, it may be very difficult for him to recover. It only takes a moment to move from doing business well to doing business unethically. When we stop being ethically aware, we're going to make mistakes, and those mistakes can be harmful.

continues ▶

This scenario could have had a happier ending if Ron had read widely in his industry (industry competence) and was aware of the dangers of arsenic in some brands of rice. If he were using ethical leadership, he would have already carefully screened his suppliers to be sure there were not dangerous levels of arsenic in the rice (ethical competence).

Having already researched safe suppliers, Ron could have picked up the phone and arranged to purchase large shipments of rice to fill the new customer's order. Making the ethical choice would have taken a bit more time, and at times it costs more, but Ron would have been building customer trust and demonstrating concern for his customers' well-being in ways that would inspire loyalty in the long run.

Competent leaders are able to recognize the skills that will be needed on the team in the future, and they learn how to lead others to successful results in the midst of change and chaos. Staying competent, as defined here, is a broad concept that includes making a commitment to be a "learning leader."

What Leaders Who Stay Competent Do

Leaders who stay competent monitor trends in and beyond their industries. They seek out new research and opinions and ideas that are different from theirs. They make learning and improving their leadership a priority, and they intentionally:

- Think ahead (in order to end up where they will need to be in the future)
- Stay on top of industry and world trends
- Stay on top of best practices in effective leadership
- Are aware of their own strengths and weaknesses
- Are committed to learning and improving
- Stay ethically aware and ethically competent
- Continually improve how they lead

Principle Four: Model Expected Performance and Leadership

Ethical leaders do not just talk a good game—they practice what they preach and are proactive role models for ethical conduct.

—Michael Brown and Linda Treviño, *Leadership Quarterly*

In an ethical culture, senior leaders establish the ethical performance, behavior, and leadership that are required throughout the organization. They teach it and they model it. They generate an open dialogue about what ethics looks like in the organization, and they hold leaders at all levels accountable for meeting expectations. No leader can be exempt from the important role of modeling the performance and leadership that is expected of others.

While top leaders are important in creating an ethical organization, leaders at all levels can make a difference by demonstrating the ethics and leadership the organization expects. Leaders who carefully consider ethics in everyday decisions let employees know that the company expects the same of them. Seeing leaders model a high level of ethical behavior helps employees manage the delicate balance between the demands of meeting ethical standards with those of meeting business goals.

According to Desmond Berghofer and Geraldine Schwartz of The Institute for Ethical Leadership, "The focus of leadership development should be on producing leaders in the middle who have personal ethical competence, who are good models for those around them, and who can empower others to get the work done in ways that promote harmony and maintain good relationships."[24]

Earning Respect by Modeling Good Performance

Because what we do sets the example for those we lead and has a powerful impact on the organization's culture, we need to consistently model ethical behavior and ethical choices. Principle Three: Stay Competent and Principle Four: Model Expected Performance and Leadership are closely related. Our success with being a good role model will depend in

47

part on how well we stay competent in our individual fields and in our leadership.

Modeling expected performance shows that we know how to do what we are asking others to do and that we know how to do it ethically. Asking others to perform according to expectations that we are not willing to follow sends a mixed message that employees usually resolve by following what they see us do rather than what we say. Jerry Brown of the Ethics Resource Center notes that "Organizational ethics becomes real for employees when they see good ethics being applied."[25]

PRINCIPLE FOUR CASE STUDY:
GOOD FOR THEM BUT NOT FOR ME

Julie, a middle manager for an executive search firm, has been very concerned about the fact that the cost of health insurance has skyrocketed. It has become a stretch for employees to make the payments. Employees have recently been asked to participate in wellness activities as a stopgap measure to reduce the overall costs of health insurance claims. Julie has told her team members how important this is and how this initiative will help the company cover the costs of its generous health insurance plan. Julie thinks the wellness initiative is a good idea, but she does not feel she has time to participate due to her leadership responsibilities. Some of her employees have proactively started walking at lunch, but Julie has declined their invitations and to date has not logged any wellness activities at all. In the next quarterly manager's meeting, each department's results are shared, and Julie is the only middle manager who has not participated. As a result, her department does not receive the participation incentives that her employees have been working hard to earn and that the other departments all receive.

OBSERVATIONS ON THE CASE

Julie has sent a mixed message to her employees about the wellness initiative. She has told them how important it is and how it will help the company continue to provide generous health insurance benefits. She has then demonstrated that it is not worthy of her time by choosing not to participate. This decision will have negative ripple effects. In addition to reducing the likelihood that employees will participate in the "next big thing" that Julie asks them to do, Julie herself:

- Is demonstrating a lack of personal congruence
- Will lose the respect of her team members who participated but did not earn incentives because of their manager's choice
- Will lose the respect of her manager and peers, who have all participated
- Will lose her credibility as someone who "walks the talk" and does what she asks others to do

These are just some of the negative effects of what was probably an "I'm just too busy" decision for Julie. We demonstrate what is important by how we use our time, and when we ask employees to do something, we need to do it too.

Leaders who are willing to do the hard jobs when help is needed earn the respect and trust of their teams. Ethical leaders who guide other leaders model every aspect of the leadership they expect from those leaders. Ethical leaders who engage workers model every aspect of the performance they expect from them. Attending required training with the team sends the message that you are learning too and that you support your individual employees and the team.

What Leaders Who Model Expected Performance and Leadership Do

Leaders who serve as good role models guide their employees toward successful performance. They demonstrate a willingness to do whatever they ask others to do, no matter how difficult or tedious the tasks may be. They ensure that they always:

- Keep their required certifications and licenses current

- Meet or exceed all performance standards required of those they lead
- Attend the full sessions of all training that is required of employees
- Periodically take a shift doing key jobs to understand the problems and questions related to the work
- Model effective and ethical leadership

Modeling the leadership and performance we expect must be built on the foundation of clear expectations for what ethical leadership looks like in our organizations. Leaders who continually stretch themselves to learn new ways of leading responsibly will be well positioned to handle increasing complexity and future challenges. Among them are the challenges of learning how to Lead in Ways That Bring Out the Best in Others, which will be discussed next in Chapter Five.

5

Lead in Ways That Bring
Out the Best in Others

*The task of leadership is not to put greatness into people
but to elicit it, for the greatness is there already.*

—John Buchan

14 Guiding Principles of Ethical Leadership

Lead With a Moral Compass	Lead in Ways That Bring Out the Best in Others
1. Demonstrate Personal Congruence	5. Respect Others
2. Be Morally Aware	6. Respect Boundaries
3. Stay Competent	7. Trust and Be Trustworthy
4. Model Expected Performance and Leadership	8. Communicate Openly
	9. Generate Effective and Ethical Performance

A s we go about leading with a moral compass, we also need to demonstrate interpersonal ethical behavior, which means respecting others, collaborating, and building trust as we fulfill our daily obligations. Principles five through nine provide detail about how to ethically fulfill our interpersonal responsibilities and how to lead for ethical and effective performance.

Principle Five: Respect Others

> *Every man is to be respected as an absolute end in himself; and it is a crime against the dignity that belongs to him as a human being, to use him as a mere means for some external purpose.*

> —Immanuel Kant

The principle of respect for others is grounded in age-old concepts that include the Golden Rule ("Do unto others as you would have them do to you"[26]); the Silver Rule ("Do not do to others the things you would not have them do to you"[27]); fair play ("We all must play by the same rules"); and the Harm Principle ("My right to swing my fist ends where the other person's nose begins"[28]). Each of these universal concepts focuses on the importance of mutuality and respect. They have been present across the world's cultures and religions through the ages, and they are the foundation of honoring basic human rights.[29]

Respecting Others

> *There can be no high civility without a deep morality.*

> —Ralph Waldo Emerson

Respecting others is a critically important part of ethical leadership for several reasons. First, it helps us get along and get things done. In their book *A Practical Guide to Ethics: Living and Leading with Integrity*,

Rita Manning and Scott Stroud conclude that "Regardless of our differences, respect for each other is both a requirement and a way of smoothing out our interactions."[30]

When we demonstrate respect, we show that we understand that other people also have life goals and that they also endure struggles as they work toward them.

Second, respecting others demonstrates that we consider others when making decisions, which is an important aspect of ethical leadership. Without respect for others, we are more likely to make decisions that benefit our self-interests and well-being at the expense of the self-interests and well-being of others.

Third, by respecting others we demonstrate awareness that we are all part of the same group—the "human group." Being a member of the "human group" comes with both rights and responsibilities. Respecting others shows that we know how to reach our goals in ways that also honor the goals of others.

"Civility" is a concept that has been gaining recent attention as an important part of moral leadership. While we may not realize that how we treat other people is a moral issue, Michael Brannigan points out that "Ethics deals fundamentally with how we treat each other on a daily basis. Indeed, our small acts of civility and incivility constitute the heart of morality."[31]

For a leader, respecting others can be as simple as listening carefully when someone speaks and as complicated as having a reliable formal system for deciding what is fair and equitable when someone's personal interests come into conflict with organizational goals.

Respecting others includes a wide range of interpersonal behaviors, such as:

- Being kind
- Being supportive
- Listening carefully to others
- Being fair and reasonable
- Demonstrating that you care
- Honoring the rights of others to have their dignity and freedom
- Considering the needs of others when making decisions

Respecting others by its nature excludes a wide variety of behaviors that include:

- Name calling
- Belittling
- Bullying
- Controlling
- Physically or verbally attacking
- Sabotaging
- Judging
- Creating unnecessary conflict

Respecting others is fundamental to ethical leadership. Because we are part of a global society, that respect needs to be intentionally extended to people who are not like us.

Respecting Differences

The surest way to corrupt a youth is to instruct him to hold in higher esteem those who think alike than those who think differently.

—Friedrich Nietzsche

Because we are a collection of unique individuals, in order to fully respect each other, we must also respect and welcome differences. John Hume, who read the inscription on Abraham Lincoln's grave and realized its importance in today's world for creating peace, said, "That summary, in three words in Latin, also written throughout America, is *E Pluribus Unum*. In other words, 'from many we are *one*' and the essence of our unity is respect for diversity."[32]

Richard Jacobs of Villanova University, describing Patrick MacLagan's work, points out that the ability to consider other viewpoints demonstrates a higher level of moral reasoning. He says, "Leaders who are not interested in listening to, do not listen to, or fail to appreciate the diversity of viewpoints and, hence, to examine the value conflicts embedded in organizational issues, demonstrate lower levels of moral reasoning than those followers who are capable of considering alternative points of view."[33]

While we may naturally be uncomfortable with people who are not like us, we must not let that discomfort lead us to an automatic judgment or fear reaction. Carl Jung said, "We cannot change anything until we accept it. Condemnation does not liberate, it oppresses."[34]

To avoid reacting automatically, respecting differences requires that we intentionally learn to become comfortable with people who are different from us. It is sometimes easier to surround ourselves with people who are just like us, but the trap is that we fail to learn and grow. Our own growth, which helps us embrace differences, depends on our interacting with a wide variety of people we don't know. Some ways that we can stretch ourselves in this area include travelling, learning to speak a world language different from our own, being involved in charitable outreach programs, and interacting with people whose approach we don't understand.

Respecting differences is fundamental to individual ethical leadership, and it is critical for organizational ethical leadership as well. When someone's personal interests come into conflict with organizational goals, it is the leader's role to help the individual and the organization think through the conflict in ways that respect others, respect differences, *and* respect organizational goals. Through respectful interpersonal behavior, we demonstrate that we:

- Are interested in what others have to say
- Are interested in their success as well as our own
- Value the unique perspectives they bring to our shared work
- Support them in achieving their potential and contributing to the success of the organization
- See them as people we can learn from
- Acknowledge that their history, views, and ideas can be different from ours in ways that provide a broader perspective for effective business and innovation

Only through full inclusion, fairness, and respect for others and differences can we build an organizational environment in which there is mutual trust and accountability.

PRINCIPLE FIVE CASE STUDY:
RESPECT IN ACTION

The marketing group of a drug store chain has a new manager from outside the company, and the employees are anxious to meet him and find out what kind of leader he is. As Carlos enters the conference room where he'll meet his team members, he greets each one individually and makes eye contact. His tone is upbeat, and he expresses interest and concern for each person in the room. It is clear to the team members that he is looking forward to getting to know them. When a receptionist has to interrupt the meeting to let him know that one more team member is finishing another meeting and is on his way, he treats the receptionist with clear respect and shows appreciation for the information. He is interested in hearing about the varied backgrounds of the team members and how they see themselves helping the group succeed. He lets the group know that he values different perspectives because they will help the team's work be fresh and innovative. His team members are relieved that he appears to be respectful and accepting of their different experiences.

The reason the marketing group has a new leader is that the previous leader did not show respect for other people or for differences. When she walked the halls in the course of her work, she only spoke with the three people who reported directly to her and pretty much ignored everyone else.

Actually, it would be more accurate to say that she ignored them until she needed something from them. Then the tone in her voice when she asked them ever-so-nicely to do something for her made her team members cringe. Her kind of respect was a "respect of convenience" only brought out when it was in her best interests to do so. Through her tone and demeanor, she showed that status mattered to her. She stayed close to upper level staff and was stingy with her words and attention with the rest of the group, seldom acknowledging the people two or more levels below her on the organizational chart.

Even worse, when there were open positions, she made it a point to look for candidates who had attended the same two or three schools that she believed best prepared marketing professionals while ignoring candidates who were interesting and had cutting-edge knowledge. Ironically, these individuals could really have helped the team in areas where fresh skills and perspectives were needed.

OBSERVATIONS ON THE CASE

In this case example, Carlos is demonstrating respect for others and respect for differences. Note that, to him, respect for others means *all* others, not just select others. His respect for differences became clear when he showed how pleased he was that the group had diverse backgrounds to bring to their work. By demonstrating such a high level of respect, Carlos will be able to quickly build trust and help his group perform its work without distraction.

The outgoing leader in this example was focused on herself and on how other people could help her rather than on how she could bring out the best in them through her leadership. By ignoring people she did not perceive to be in power, she demonstrated a low level of maturity and a lack of interpersonal ethical leadership.

Leaders who respect others do a variety of things that demonstrate they are interested in others, care about others, and want to learn from others. They honor the dignity and rights of all people. They are not afraid of lively discussions that include different perspectives, and in fact they value that type of exchange because it is engaging and makes the team better.

What Leaders Who Respect Others Do

Leaders who respect others demonstrate the highest civility and respect in all of their daily interactions. They respect each individual's rights, and they honor collective human rights. They show care and concern for everyone regardless of status in the organization or status in life. They welcome divergent viewpoints and backgrounds and enjoy learning from others who see the world differently. Such leaders intentionally:

- Value and seek out a variety of perspectives
- Build diverse teams
- Help teammates work together collaboratively
- Demonstrate interest, care, and concern for all others in all that they do
- Respect all types of people, at all levels, and in all positions
- Support employees to bring out their best and achieve individual and group success
- Require respectful behavior
- Remove stressors and other barriers to success
- Actively learn from others without regard for their status

Principle Six: Respect Boundaries

Morality, like art, means drawing a line someplace.

—Oscar Wilde

Respect for boundaries is related to the broad principle of "respect for others." It is presented here as a separate principle because this special kind of respect can be especially important in the workplace. Ethical leaders are aware of spoken and unspoken boundaries and are careful to set and honor boundaries for the kinds of behavior that are acceptable. The culture of each organization is different, so no one set of boundary rules can apply everywhere, but regardless of what the rules may be, it is the leader's responsibility to ensure they are clear, explicit, understandable, and mutually respected.

Drawing the Line

A shorthand way of thinking about a boundary is to consider where you would draw the line about something. To clarify why boundaries are important in organizations, I will look at several examples of boundaries that draw lines around acceptable and unacceptable behavior. These include:

- Time and place boundaries (understandings about how a given behavior is appropriate at certain times and places but not at others)
- Environmental boundaries (limits on levels of noise, lighting, safety hazards, etc.)
- Personal and relationship boundaries (understandings about another's privacy needs and maintaining appropriate interpersonal behavior)
- Informational boundaries (protecting personal and organizational confidentiality and proprietary information)
- Property and rights boundaries (honoring the property and rights of others)
- Scope-of-work boundaries (mutual understanding about whether or not it is appropriate to cross into others' assigned projects or job descriptions)

If we think of our role as the "hat" we wear, we can conceptualize boundaries as where we should draw the line when wearing that particular hat. Appropriate boundaries are not the same for every "hat" we might wear. For example, the level of intimacy I have with my spouse and children is not appropriate when I am wearing my leader hat at work.

Within any workplace, different roles may require different boundaries. For example, regarding informational boundaries and confidentiality, the CEO and human resources manager need to refrain from discussing private information about employees, even if they are in situations where others are discussing it. There are also basic workplace boundaries that apply across the entire organization regardless of the roles or "hats" involved. For example, gossiping about other employees should be considered universally out of bounds. There should also be limits to allowed noise levels, with certain limitations necessary for safety purposes, and so on.

Some boundaries will be imposed from the highest level of leadership, while others may be negotiable and responsive to employee opinions. A senior leadership team setting a boundary that forbids employees from accessing certain websites from office computers would be an example of an imposed boundary. The boundary would be designed to keep people focused on their work and to maintain a level of professionalism.

By contrast, a department leader dealing with disagreements about music choices and volume levels in a shared work space could manage that as a negotiable boundary and accept input from group members. This boundary would be designed to prevent conflict and to ensure that everyone is able to concentrate on their work.

Certain boundary rules may vary from one context to another within the same organization. For example, it may be acceptable in the sales department to eat at one's desk, but that may not be permitted in the graphic design studio, where food could ruin the camera-ready proofs.

Regardless of the type of boundary, or how and where the decisions are made, leaders are responsible for establishing and communicating clear and understandable rules about boundaries, modeling the behavior that is expected, providing training about the expected behavior in various contexts, being physically present in various settings often enough to monitor whether these expectations are being met, and respectfully enforcing those rules and boundaries.

Time and Place Boundaries

What specific behaviors are appropriate (or inappropriate) in different work settings? Leaders sometimes fail to clarify that different contexts require different behavior. A simplistic example is that the behavior and dress code that was considered appropriate at the company picnic on Saturday will likely not be appropriate in Monday's board meeting; and the language and tone used at the company's weekend ball game may not be appropriate in the weekday workplace.

Where the line is drawn about such things as dress will depend upon the company culture and will vary greatly across organizations. There may be a "dress-down" code to match the informal atmosphere of a small information technology company, whereas there may be a "dress-up" code to match the professional climate in an established law firm. The boundaries within the workplace may also vary depending upon whether the public will be entering the workplace as prospective clients or customers. In some companies, uniforms may be provided and required. In others, where there is a relatively formal atmosphere, employees may enjoy casual Fridays as an exception to the regular dress code. In some organizations, employees can be encouraged to participate in deciding where the lines will be drawn about behavior and dress. In others, these decisions will need to be made from above.

When could setting time and place boundaries have ethical implications? Here are two examples:

- A leader is asked to consider exceptions to attendance rules when employees want to participate in religious observances. Allowing this time off demonstrates respect for others and respect for differences, but the leader also needs to be consistent and fair in managing special requests within the whole group to be sure that some employees are not provided with significantly more time off than others.

- A leader has to decide whether to hold the annual sales recognition dinner at a local restaurant chain or at a sports bar that features waitresses in skimpy outfits. The employees are mostly male, but this does not matter in choosing a setting that demonstrates respect for others, respect for differences (both men and women), and appropriate professionalism.

Environmental Boundaries

How will we share space in ways that demonstrate respect and courtesy for others? How will we use our workspace in ways that enhance employee satisfaction and productivity? Although the decision-making process about environmental boundaries can include requesting opinions and recommendations from all employees, sometimes decisions need to be made from above. It is important that leaders demonstrate their final decision-making authority after hearing from team members, because these boundaries can have an impact on workplace morale, productivity, and safety.

Boundaries about noise levels can include such things as guidelines about whether employees are allowed to bring their own music into the workplace when it will affect others (as when it is played "into the air" or broadcast as background music) or could affect safety (as when employees are allowed to wear headphones or ear buds that might impair their ability to hear important instructions).

Lighting decisions can also be complicated. Will the most inexpensive florescent lighting make everyone's complexion look abnormal and therefore affect morale? Will the chosen lighting flicker in a way that risks triggering seizures in certain employees? Will employees with visual difficulties be allowed to bring in supplemental lighting for their own work space? If so, must the company engineer pass judgment on the safety of that equipment before it is installed?

Personal and Relationship Boundaries

What personal and relationship boundaries should guide our work? These can be among the most difficult boundaries to create and enforce. For example, when it comes to personal boundaries and physical touch, everyone would agree that certain behaviors would always be inappropriate at work (e.g., hitting or punching, physical intimacy, or sexual gestures). But there are many grey areas about interpersonal physical behavior.

Each employee will enter the corporation with a slightly different personal history and cultural background that affects what they consider to be appropriate. For example, do they believe it is appropriate to physically touch others without first obtaining their permission (for example, initiating a pat on the shoulder or a hug)? Do they believe it is acceptable to use intimate language like nicknames and terms of endearment?

Leaders' decisions about where the line will be drawn regarding personal and relationship boundaries must take into account not only their own personal values and the company's values but also risk-management considerations and relevant laws. For this reason, although they can elicit employee input, leaders must take final responsibility for determining and enforcing the appropriate boundaries.

Informational Boundaries

When are employees free to disclose personal information about someone else within the corporation? No workplace culture should foster or tolerate gossip and backbiting among employees, but beyond these things, what are the other expectations about the extent to which employees will maintain confidentiality and privacy? Is it appropriate to discuss each other's personal business outside the workplace? Is this an area of concern or not? Will employees themselves participate in making decisions about it? The answers will vary from one context to another, but it is up to leaders to set and monitor information boundaries that honor personal privacy and confidentiality.

When are employees free to disclose information about the company's plans and products? This decision must come from upper leadership. Every company should have clear rules about the disclosure of proprietary information, but are there also other aspects of company information that employees should be expected to keep confidential? If so, these should be explicitly clarified.

One important clarification involves whether employees will be prohibited from sharing certain information on social media websites. This could include everything from the company's private plans to confidential communications. For corporations involved in inventing and patenting certain products or processes, it would be appropriate for rules about this to be included in the personnel manual and the hiring contract, with the stipulation that failure to follow the established policies will potentially result in termination of employment.

Property and Rights Boundaries

How will we respect what doesn't belong to us? Respecting the property of others includes big things like not trespassing, not stealing, and not plagiarizing content. It also includes small things such as not "borrowing" from other people's snacks and lunches in the break room refrigerator without asking.

How will we respect the rights of others? Respecting rights includes honoring human rights and not interfering with other people's well-being, success, or happiness. It also includes not harming or threatening to harm.

Scope-of-Work Boundaries

How will we divide up projects and collaborate to get them done? Organizations are free to create their own "scope-of-work" rules. Boundaries in this area balance expectations about job descriptions, when to limit work, and when to collaborate with each other in getting work done. Decisions about how to divide up projects and how to work together to get them done will depend upon the size of the organization as well as its prevailing culture. Lack of leadership and clarity about scope of work boundaries can lead to misunderstandings among employees.

For example, are employees expected to volunteer to consult with a fellow employee if they believe she needs help solving a problem or is at risk for missing a deadline? Should fellow employees give this individual all the help they can, or should they take their concerns to management? Routinely setting and honoring the types of boundaries described here helps us build group trust and ensures that employees understand the invisible but important boundaries that should guide them in their various roles and responsibilities.

PRINCIPLE SIX CASE STUDY:
CALLING AT DINNER TIME

David is a supervisor at a telemarketing firm that specializes in raising money for charities. He believes it is acceptable to raise money for the firm's non-profit clients by calling at dinnertime, early in the morning, and after 9:00 p.m., when people expect only family members and friends to call. The law currently allows such calls, but there is word the law will be changing soon.

David is asked by two of his charity clients to stop making the intrusive calls now, to demonstrate good faith and to adapt to the coming change in the laws that regulate telemarketing. David isn't willing to give up the bonuses he earns for bringing in so much money, even if it is accomplished through a less than respectful approach. A short time later, in a single week, four long-time clients tell David they are going to use someone else to raise money for their charities.

OBSERVATIONS ON THE CASE

Even if it is legal to call at intrusive times without an invitation, it is inappropriate. David is not considering how important it is for families to spend uninterrupted time together at dinnertime, before school, and at children's bedtimes. Even though David is single, he should respect typical family schedules and limit calls to times generally thought to be appropriate in the industry. By trying to squeeze out the extra bit of profit made by inconveniencing others, he ends up losing four bread-and-butter clients. Those clients realize that it is unethical for David to continue what he is doing, especially since the laws will soon be changing. Ethical leaders balance profitability with concern for others and consider the long-term impact of their choices.

Leaders who respect boundaries make sure that workplace guidelines are fair, clear, and understood and that everyone follows them. They realize that the boundaries that govern their actions change as they change roles.

What Leaders Who Respect Boundaries Do

Leaders who respect boundaries:
- Set and communicate performance boundaries for employees
- Honor all appropriate boundaries in their own work
- Maintain confidentiality (and transparency) where appropriate
- Prevent gossip, blaming, backbiting, teasing, and other disrespectful interpersonal behaviors
- Manage noise levels, physical space allocations, and other environmental factors in ways that are fair and that allow all employees to do their best work
- Communicate clearly and model what the boundaries are for events and day-to-day work (for example, casual Fridays but business dress for client meetings)
- Manage boundaries in predictable ways that build trust within the group and the organization
- Balance the need for profitability with a demonstrated concern for the well-being of others

Principle Seven: Trust and Be Trustworthy

The ethical obligation is to live one's life so as to be worthy of trust.

—Michael Josephson, Josephson Institute

Stephen M. R. Covey in *The Speed of Trust* shares his belief that "The ability to establish, grow, extend and restore trust is not only vital to our personal and interpersonal well-being; it is the key leadership competency of the new global economy."[35]

In order to create an environment in which people can contribute according to their potential, a leader must care about others, trust others to do their part, and behave in ways that earn trust from others.

Demonstrate Care

People generally tend to trust others who have a sincere concern and compassion for other people. We trust people who care—about us and their interactions with us, how well they treat us, our well-being, our personal goals, our individual and group learning, and other aspects of "care."

Care has also emerged as a major issue in ethical leadership research. Western Kentucky University shares this definition: "A care ethic de-emphasizes the idea of the independent individual and instead stresses that persons exist in a web of relationships."[36]

With a care ethic, leaders choose behaviors that support others and consider the well-being of a wide variety of constituents. Without a care ethic, a leader is more apt to make decisions based on individual goals and values and to ignore the impact of those choices on others. Caring for others widens the range of variables we consider when making decisions to include the other people in our organizations, communities, and societies.

Trust Others to Do Their Part

He who does not trust enough, will not be trusted.

—Lao Tzu

One of the basic philosophies of people who generate trust in organizations is that they begin by assuming positive intent. They start by assuming that people have the organization's best interests at heart and have good reasons for doing what they're doing. This view helps them avoid jumping to conclusions when something seems "different" about the way someone is behaving. Instead of blaming or taking over, a leader who initially assumes positive intent will ask an employee why a certain action was taken and will listen in order to learn rather than judge.

Behave in Ways That Earn Trust From Others

Not all behaviors are equal in the workplace. Some behaviors support good work and others don't. Behaving in ways that earn trust from others overlaps with Principle 1: Demonstrate Personal Congruence because it involves being sincere and consistent and living up to your promises. In fact, most, if not all, of the 14 Guiding Principles, when demonstrated by leaders, help them build trust.

The kinds of behaviors trustworthy leaders use include:

- Listening
- Supporting
- Showing respect for others
- Demonstrating random acts of kindness
- Showing appreciation
- Working for the greater good of the group, the company, and society
- Building united groups
- Innovating together
- Sharing credit for successes
- Taking responsibility for failures

Conversely, leaders whose groups find them difficult to trust may be using these behaviors:

- Judging
- Merely tolerating others who are different
- Instigating conflict

- Verbally attacking
- Name calling
- Bullying
- Belittling
- Sabotaging
- Blaming others for failures
- Acting out of greed and self-interest
- Posturing
- Taking credit for group successes

Build Group Trust

Groups with trustworthy leaders appreciate the special way they encourage group members to have a positive shared experience while getting the work done. Group-building leadership behaviors that encourage trust include:

- Clarifying the mission, vision, and values
- Clarifying roles and responsibilities
- Clarifying performance expectations
- Setting priorities based on the mission, vision, and values
- Sharing information readily (while honoring information boundaries)
- Building diverse and collaborative project teams
- Encouraging people to support each other
- Solving group problems and removing barriers to success
- Engaging all employees in working toward the group's shared success
- Celebrating milestones and learning from failures

Group-building behaviors that discourage trust include:

- Trying to be all things to all people without clear priorities
- Giving vague assignments that overlap
- Enforcing unstated performance expectations (that may change without notice)
- Holding information closely (that is needed by the team)

- Giving assignments to individuals and not encouraging people to support each other
- Making all of the decisions independently
- Failing to express appreciation for contributions to group success

PRINCIPLE SEVEN CASE STUDY:
PLANNED REDUNDANCY

Both of the leaders who report to a certain transportation company senior vice president know that group life can be complicated and sometimes chaotic. The leader who has been there the longest, Max, likes to "stir the pot" to make his day more interesting. He sets up complicated situations where workers are doing the same things and don't discover it right away and where pieces of negative information are "leaked" to generate confusion and distress among team members. His team is frustrated, angry, and generally afraid of what he might do next. As a leader, he is not trusted, and because he pits employees against one another, they do not trust each other, either. The department is struggling to provide services to clients, since they are expending so much energy managing the internal chaos and negative interpersonal dynamics.

Because he is working against productive performance, acting in untrustworthy ways, and intentionally eroding trust within the group, Max is an unethical leader. The organization will have to quickly work with Max to help him change his behavior and his leadership or the performance problems he has created in his group may spread throughout the rest of the company.

The newer leader, Sadie, has taken great care to build trust within her team and to act in trustworthy ways. People know they can come to her anytime they have a problem. Beyond being supportive, she also finds ways to engage the group in solving those problems so they'll know how to solve them on their own in the future. Her goal is to have everyone performing at the highest level possible, and then to stretch that ability to new levels individually and as a group.

continues ▶

Sadie's team never has problems filling open positions. The reputation of the team is stellar and employees enjoy their work. Sadie is seen as a highly ethical leader and is asked to join a company-wide task force that is reviewing ethical codes and standards for the company.

OBSERVATIONS ON THE CASE

In this case, Max has violated many of the principles of ethical leadership. He is not demonstrating respect for others (principle five). He is not behaving in trustworthy ways or trusting his group members (principle seven). He is communicating selectively, not openly (principle eight), and he is not generating ethical and effective performance (principle nine).

These problems may stem from the fact that Max is not morally aware (principle two) or is not staying competent as a leader (principle three). Regardless of the cause, leaders like Max harm organizations.

Leaders who trust and are trustworthy begin by assuming that people will be trustworthy and treat them accordingly. They do the big and small day-to-day things that make employees feel respected and valued.

What Leaders Who Trust and Are Trustworthy Do

Leaders who trust and are trustworthy begin by assuming that people have good intentions and want to do good work. They balance that assumption with a keen awareness of risk, but this awareness is quiet and in the background, like radar. It is easy to see that trustworthy leaders:

- Have a sincere concern and compassion for others
- Readily share information, work, and power
- Behave in ways that build trust
- Expect trustworthy behavior from everyone they lead
- Actively extend trust to others, beginning with the assumption that others have positive intentions
- Actively build trust within the group, encouraging people to help and support each other

Principle Eight: Communicate Openly

Communication leads to community, that is, to understanding,
intimacy and mutual valuing.

—Rollo May

Open, strategic communication has a powerful impact on the ability of individuals and groups to accomplish good work. The concept of open leadership communication is equally about *what* is communicated and *how* communication is implemented. Employees need to know what they are to focus on and how they are to go about doing their work. They need to be aware of the work other team members are doing and how to handle complicated situations.

What is communicated to a work group needs to include:

- The mission and vision of the organization and how the group directly supports it
- Performance expectations, including ethical behavior
- Who is working on each project, who is supporting these individuals, and the timeline for completion
- Dialogue about balancing strategy, ethics, effectiveness, and results
- Focusing on what you want more of (the positive) rather than focusing on what you don't want (the negative)
- Successes to repeat and failures to avoid repeating
- Overall progress of the group toward its mission and vision

How communication is implemented needs to include:

- Transparency
- Accessibility and availability to answer questions
- Listening attentively in order to facilitate understanding
- Open discussion of any business subjects
- Being polite and still saying what should be said[37]
- Sincerity and humility rather than doing things to garner attention[38]

- Collaborative communication rather than top-down proclamations
- Openness to feedback, both positive and negative
- Mastering current social channels of communication and using them to respond to customers and communities

Open and honest communication is respectful of others (principle five) and builds trust (principle seven). It also goes a long way toward building an ethical workplace where people can do their very best work (principle nine).

Why do we need to use social media channels in communication? One reason is that it is important to stay competent (principle three) as the world changes. Social media is how we communicate now, how customers let us know what they need, how they engage with our brands, and how they share product reviews and advice. While it can be a challenge to leap into social media in the beginning, in the long run, I discovered that it shortened my research time and helped me stay in meaningful ongoing conversations with my colleagues and clients.

PRINCIPLE EIGHT CASE STUDY:
HIDDEN INFORMATION

Raj and Melissa both lead groups in the operations division of a regional bank. When the vice president of operations communicates a new project to them on a Friday to share with their employees, they take very different approaches. Raj chooses to write a memo about the new project explaining what the vice president shared with him. He notes in the memo that he is available for questions. He hands it out on a Friday and plans to discuss it in a meeting on Monday.

Raj's employees become concerned over the weekend about how the news will affect them. Will anyone have to scrap current projects? Will there be additional funds available to get the work done? The project is in a new geographical area, and employees wonder if their jobs are safe. Will they need new training? Will there be overtime? By Monday, the group is exhausted from running scenarios in their heads and reluctant to discuss the new project when Raj opens up the floor for questions.

Melissa takes a different approach, deciding to call a brief meeting of her staff on Friday to discuss the project and how it will impact the team. She is able to answer most questions on the spot and agrees to go back to the vice president of operations to get answers to the remaining questions. Melissa's team feels involved and relaxed as they head into the weekend. On Monday, they have only minor questions and they are ready to start making detailed plans for completing the project.

OBSERVATIONS ON THE CASE

Melissa used open communication to involve her group and demonstrated concern for their feelings by dealing with the information quickly, before they heard about it from anyone else. This demonstrated respect (principle five) and built trust (principle seven). The group could focus on the success of the project and not worry about unknown variables, which also supported organizational effectiveness (principle nine).

Raj's decision to handle the communication in a memo left his team worried about what he *wasn't* saying. Team members wasted a lot of time and energy expressing their concerns to each other and wondering out loud what it all meant. A short meeting with open communication could have left them feeling involved in the process as they went home for the weekend.

What Leaders Who Communicate Openly Do

Leaders who communicate openly realize that people do better work when they have the information they need. Accordingly, they share as much information as they can. They also respect boundaries in choosing what to communicate and how to convey it. Such leaders:

- See the value in having an informed and empowered group
- Clearly communicate expectations, focusing on the desired behaviors

- Readily share information while at the same time respecting the boundaries of confidentiality, appropriateness, and timing
- Are transparent in their dealings with others, making it easy to get good work done
- Encourage open dialogue within the group
- Discuss work issues that employees want to discuss and provide guidance where needed

Principle Nine: Generate Effective and Ethical Performance

Ethics and effectiveness go hand in hand.

—Joanne Ciulla

Generating effective and ethical performance involves many overlapping responsibilities. To accomplish it, we need to apply all eight of the 14 Guiding Principles we've discussed so far:

Lead With a Moral Compass
Principle One: Demonstrate Personal Congruence
Principle Two: Be Morally Aware
Principle Three: Stay Competent
Principle Four: Model Expected Performance and Leadership

Lead in Ways That Bring Out the Best in Others
Principle Five: Respect Others
Principle Six: Respect Boundaries
Principle Seven: Trust and Be Trustworthy
Principle Eight: Communicate Openly

In addition to fulfilling the responsibilities discussed in principles one through eight, ethical leaders also engage employees in meaningful work while making ethics a priority. Doing both simultaneously helps create an ethical culture in which people can do good work and experience a sense of pride in their accomplishments.

Think back to an ethical leader you had the privilege to work with and remember the sense of pride you felt about the group's work. Ethical leaders have a way of making hard work fun and ethical choices seem easy and clear. This creates a strong bond and a shared sense of meaning within the groups they lead.

Engaging and Motivating Employees

How do we best engage employees for high performance? Research now shows that giving piecemeal rewards for accomplishments can actually de-motivate people. The standard formula for motivating people with punishments and rewards ignores what Daniel Pink describes as "the third drive," or "The deeply human need to direct our own lives, to learn and create new things, and to do better by ourselves and our world."[39]

With this definition in mind, generating ethical performance requires that we enable the success of our employees and then let them "own" and direct their work. The following leadership approaches, when used in combination with the 14 Guiding Principles explained in this book, generally help motivate people:

1. Encouraging cooperation, not competition
2. Encouraging people to work on what they are most interested in that fits the business purpose
3. Helping people reach their performance goals and their own potential
4. Enabling employees to direct their own work
5. Sharing ownership
6. Innovating to keep work current and meaningful
7. Being transparent while honoring information boundaries including confidentiality
8. Staying focused on the vision and mission of the organization
9. Applying resources to the greatest strategic priorities
10. Staying true to the group's values
11. Making ethics a priority

Making Ethics a Priority

Ethical organizations generally perform better than other organizations. One reason is that ethical leadership builds trust, and in a high-trust environment, employees can easily bring their full potential to their work. Another reason is that ethical organizations intentionally engage employees in meaningful work and involve them in improving the communities they serve.

Making ethics a priority helps generate effective and ethical performance and includes the following leadership responsibilities (see also the section in Chapter Eight called "Managing Ethics As a System"):

- Setting clear ethical expectations
- Intentionally building an ethical culture
- Generating open dialogue grounded in ethical values
- Helping leaders learn what "ethical" means in day-to-day work
- Providing opportunities for people to practice making ethical decisions and identifying ethical behaviors
- Rewarding and talking about ethical choices
- Sharing what is learned from ethical failures
- Having clear work policies and boundaries
- Having an ethics code

PRINCIPLE NINE CASE STUDY: LEFT IN THE DUST

Jack is a marketing professional who reports to Angela. Angela has not kept up with changes in the marketing field, and her failure to adapt is beginning to hurt the bottom line. She is of the opinion that expanding the firm's use of social media channels will take time away from getting work done. She has not seen the latest research that shows social media is the future, that it's how customers want to communicate, and that it's how they choose products and services. She doesn't realize this is how savvy firms find their customers and engage them in making buying decisions.

At Angela's last staff meeting, Jack pointed out that they were being "left in the dust" by firms with less experience who had jumped onto social media forums. He shared that he thought the last three proposals the firm submitted were rejected because they used outdated marketing methods and did not incorporate social media channels beyond LinkedIn, Twitter, and Facebook. Before that meeting, Angela had already noticed that her team was not excited about their work anymore, and she was considering hiring a consultant to help fix the problem.

OBSERVATIONS ON THE CASE

Angela is noticing a problem with morale and engagement on her team, but she hasn't yet connected it to the fact that she has refused to keep up with social channels of communication. Employees who are active in social media easily see the competence gap in their leaders who don't adapt to using it.

Staff members often know what needs to be done to keep work current and to keep employees motivated. When they suggest solutions, we need to listen deeply and respond quickly. Often, it is our own failure to adapt as leaders that worsens motivation problems. Employees want more than good work. They want meaning. They want to be valued, listened to, and involved in making the company the best that it can be. A leader keeps people focused on the most important work and guides their professional development. For these reasons, when a leader fails to stay competent (principle three), the performance of the whole group suffers.

What Leaders Who Manage Effective and Ethical Performance Do

Leaders who manage effective and ethical performance balance the competing demands of efficiency, effectiveness, and ethics. They keep up with trends and help their teams stay ahead of the changes that will affect their work. They build high-trust environments in which employees enjoy learning, collaborating, and discovering innovative solutions to problems.

Such leaders:

- Model expected performance in all areas
- Stay competent
- Encourage people to follow their interests within the business mission
- Provide the opportunity for employees to direct their own work
- Support employees who are learning
- Encourage collaboration
- Listen to and value all employees
- Involve employees in making key decisions that affect their work
- Innovate to stay current and keep work meaningful

The five principles explored in Chapter Five focus on leading others ethically. In Chapter Six, I move to a higher level view of ethical leadership to look at leading ethically in a connected society, exploring three more important principles that relate to how we think and act as leaders. Together, these principles convey the importance of positive intent and impact.

Lead With Positive Intent and Impact

Ethical intent surely requires self-forgetfulness as well as self-awareness.

—Robin Downie, Glasgow University

14 Guiding Principles of Ethical Leadership

Lead With a Moral Compass	Lead in Ways That Bring Out the Best in Others
1. Demonstrate Personal Congruence 2. Be Morally Aware 3. Stay Competent 4. Model Expected Performance and Leadership	5. Respect Others 6. Respect Boundaries 7. Trust and Be Trustworthy 8. Communicate Openly 9. Generate Effective and Ethical Performance
	Lead With Positive Intent and Impact 10. Think Like an Ethical Leader 11. Do Good Without Doing Harm 12. Work for Mutually Beneficial Solutions

D r. Rushworth Kidder, founder of the Institute for Global Ethics, wrote in *There's Only Ethics*, "We will not survive the 21st century with the ethics of the 20th century. Something significant has to change."[40]

While the basic responsibilities of leading people are constant, the world has changed in ways that now require us to navigate through a web of issues and expectations. In Chapter One, I talked about the challenge of preparing leaders to handle complexity and make ethical choices. As the complexity of work increases and our diverse collection of nations becomes more interdependent, we need to keep up with the changing context in which we lead.

The ways we think about leading ethically need to be broad enough to help us make ethical choices in such a rapidly changing context. They need to be other-focused enough to guide us to serve and support others and avoid causing harm. They need to be positive and proactive enough to guide us to do good. And they need to be specific enough to help us know what to do and what not to do. Principles ten, eleven, and twelve help us make ethical choices within this rapidly changing leadership context.

Principle Ten: Think Like an Ethical Leader

What a peculiar privilege has this little
agitation of the brain which we call "thought."

—David Hume

John Maxwell points out in his book *Today Matters* that "thinking precedes achievement."[41] To make our ethical leadership journey successful, we must intentionally choose to use the kind of thinking that leads to ethical choices and behavior. It's important for us to realize that some common thinking practices do not lead us in the direction of ethical leadership.

Levels of Thinking That Do Not
Necessarily Lead to Ethical Leadership

Commonly used levels of thinking do not generally lead to ethical solutions. These include making decisions only at the "gut" level, basing decisions on legal standards alone, or making choices based solely on personal or company values. Below, I explore each of these three common approaches that do not provide a sufficiently broad view of the context to help us make ethical choices.

The Gut Level

Making decisions "from the gut" is not guaranteed to lead us to ethical choices. Unless we have completely internalized the principles of managing complexity and leading ethically, gut-level decisions can easily lead us astray. This is because they don't always take into consideration enough of the important variables. If I follow only my gut reaction when I meet someone new, for example, it means I react to this individual's appearance and the few words he or she speaks. While these things do provide some information, they don't convey the depth of this individual's experience, values, or intentions. Many times in my life, someone my gut told me I wouldn't like working with turned out to be someone I learned valuable lessons from.

For some people who have highly developed ethical principles, it can be helpful to begin the decision-making process by noticing one's "gut reaction," but that is only the beginning. Jonathan Baron, in his article "A Psychological View of Moral Intuition," said, "If we want to understand morality, our intuitions are not enough, although as a guide to behavior they may be very good."[42] Regardless of how good our "ethical intuition" may be, it is important to evaluate our gut reaction by engaging in a more structured decision-making process that takes into account relevant variables and potential consequences.

LAWS

As I discussed in Chapter Three, laws are the minimum standard and are not intended to represent "best practices" in ethical leadership. While following the law is important, using legal standards as the only basis for ethical leadership is a mistake since such standards represent the level below which leaders are punished for their unethical actions. There are several reasons why following laws does not lead us to ethical leadership:

- Laws do not change quickly enough to adapt to the changes in our world
- Laws are specific rather than systemic so they focus on one area, sometimes in isolation, without consideration of other variables that should impact the decision
- Many things that are technically "legal" for business leaders to do are now considered completely inappropriate and can still get a business into trouble

For example, bullying is not acceptable behavior in current society. Laws are beginning to change to reflect that, but the fact that your state may not yet have such a law does not make it acceptable to bully or to allow bullying in your company. Aiming at the level of following laws and regulations may keep you out of jail, but it won't make you an ethical leader. Instead, imagine that laws are the ethical floor (the bottom level) and the ethical leadership described in this book is the ceiling (the level to reach for).

PERSONAL AND ORGANIZATIONAL VALUES

Why wouldn't basing decisions on individual ethical values necessarily lead to ethical decisions? Making decisions solely based on your personal values—or on one value alone—may cause your decision to conflict with what good ethical principles require in the situation. Sometimes good business leadership calls upon value distinctions that do not ordinarily come into play in one's personal life. The risk is high—a leader's individual values, perspectives, and ethics influence the boundaries of ethical workplace behavior and can have wide-ranging consequences.

For some leaders, decisions based on their own personal values may be inappropriately skewed toward profitability to the exclusion of other important variables. For example, a company led by a leader who values profitability above all may choose a chemical additive that protects freshness and is cheap to buy and may keep using it even when that chemical is found to cause harm to human health.

Another risk of using only individual and/or company values is that doing so may lead to an oversimplified decision-making process. Sometimes senior leaders make selected values paramount rather than balancing the needs of stakeholders and considering the organization's broader impact on the system in which the organization operates (this includes employees, communities, the country, the planet, and the long-term greater good). When this happens, leaders may make short-sighted and damaging decisions. For example, a "Customer is always right" value places a burden on employees to meet excessive demands and may strain the resources of the organization in meeting those needs. Likewise a "Put people first" value is great for the organization's people, but isn't environmental impact important too?

While they are not effective as the only factor in decision making, individual and organizational values can be helpful. They guide us as we choose the most important places to avoid harm when using ethical principles to make decisions, but they are not enough. The context is too complex and the possible impact too connected for each leader to use only individual and company values to make decisions.

The Impact of Biases and Assumptions

To be sure that we are using ethical thinking, we need to continually check our biases and assumptions. Our brains use assumptions as "shortcuts" when making decisions, and we are not always fully aware of them.

Here are some questions to consider about our biases and assumptions:

- Has a bad experience with one person programmed me to automatically assume that everyone from that country (or religion, race, etc.) is bad?

- Do I respect entire groups of people less because of what one person did?
- Have I made an assumption that has become a judgment that is impacting my behavior?
- Does how I am behaving violate Principle Five: Respect Others?

At a recent speaker series event at the University of Richmond, I sat with a group of people I had not met before. Over lunch, we talked about current issues. One of the most articulate and interesting people at the table also had a nose ring and multiple ear piercings.

We all have a tendency to want to categorize people based on their appearance, background, beliefs, or lifestyle. That's one way we make sense of the world. The problem is that we miss a great deal when we label and judge people before we get to know them. Intentionally becoming aware of how our biases and assumptions impact our decisions is important in ethical decision making. Our thinking helps us determine how to handle situations, and we need to be sure that we are fully aware of, and in charge of, our thinking.

A Better Alternative: A Systems View

How can we learn to evaluate ethical decisions broadly enough to reflect what really happens in the world? While the decision-making approaches we have reviewed so far (gut levels, based on laws alone, and individual and organizational values) do not necessarily lead to ethical choices, there is an approach that more often does.

A systems view is a way of thinking that considers the connections among multiple variables and constituents; it is a way to understand multiple interdependent variables and to make informed decisions. When we make decisions based on ethical principles and the connected nature of systems, we look beyond our own values and can be surer that those values are not blinding us and keeping us from seeing other important variables.

Thinking with a systems view considers all the other levels (including the gut level, laws and values, and individual and company values) and many other variables that need to be considered for ethical decision making.

This perspective allows today's leaders a wider view, an understanding of connected, evolving variables, and an approach to making decisions that provides mutual benefit.

Without a systems view, we make decisions based on our own frames of reference and on our individually preferred levels of thinking (mentioned above) without considering the impact of those choices on others and the environment over time. This means we cannot fully evaluate the ethical impact of our choices, and it can lead us to put ourselves, our employees, our customers, and our organizations at risk.

Unfortunately, many leaders have not yet mastered thinking at the systems level of leadership. Even our definitions of "effective leadership" can limit our thinking. For example, leadership books tend to focus on specific individual functions of effective leadership rather than on the difficult task of balancing those functions effectively. I could quote from my preferred leadership book to make the case for many decisions that end up being bad ones from a systems perspective. Using systems thinking, effective and ethical leaders get a broader view of situations before trying to resolve them.

We need to be able to handle ethical grey areas in our daily work quickly and well. These grey areas are emerging faster than resources to handle them can be published, and there will not be guidelines that explain how to make decisions for every single messy, complicated situation we find ourselves in. Systems thinking gives us the tools to work through these difficult situations responsibly and effectively.

Layers of Connecting Systems

Leadership is not a one-person game. After all, if no one is following, we can't conclude that anyone is leading.[43] Leadership involves interactions between leaders and followers in which each participant is affected by all the others. These interactions do not occur in a vacuum; they create a third entity which is an interpersonal system. Each participant in the system affects all the others, while the very system the participants create affects everyone in it. Because of this ongoing "feedback loop," organizational systems are constantly in motion, making it difficult for leaders to see all the moving parts clearly.

This network of interpersonal systems that make up organizations also must operate in the context of the organization's performance management system. In other words, the leader/follower interactions take place within the boundaries of the organization's performance and leadership standards. These related systems and many others operate within the external context of industry regulation and governance and so on.

Systems thinking helps us see patterns and cycles and to understand the full picture. Cause-and-effect thinking, by contrast, almost always has unintended consequences, whereas systems thinking leads to better decisions in several ways:

- It avoids short-term narrow thinking
- It connects diverse areas of leadership responsibility
- It includes more of what we need to be thinking about
- It considers the long-term implications, not just the short-term rewards

A Service Mindset and a Global View

The high destiny of the individual is to serve rather than to rule.

—Albert Einstein

Are we in leadership positions for the purpose of serving ourselves? Clearly, we are not. Using a service mindset in leadership means that we dedicate ourselves to the service of those we lead and to the service of our customers and communities. A service mindset requires a posture of humility. As leaders, our role is to help others succeed, not just to make sure we ourselves succeed.

Because the impact of our leadership will not be limited only to the confines of our buildings and boundaries, we need to consider our impact in the broadest possible context—on a global scale. Demonstrating globally responsible leadership is important for every leader, regardless of the size or scope of the business they lead. The decisions we make have a ripple effect that can either be positive or negative. Those ripples travel fast in a networked world.

We are leading in a globally connected society, and that requires global thinking and global citizenship. Whether or not we lead a global company, we need to be thinking about our impact on the global community. Systems thinking helps us see connections, and a global view helps us consider those connections on a global scale. In our connected society, ethical leaders need to make sure their thinking includes a service mindset and a global view.

PRINCIPLE TEN CASE STUDY: TAKING THE COMPANY BY STORM

Lisa has recently been hired by a software firm to lead a project management team. Her resume is stellar, and she has the kind of experience the firm requires for the position. By her third week on the job, though, it becomes clear that she is not using the kind of leadership thinking that builds positive relationships. In a recent meeting where she was asked to share resources with another team on a joint project, she refused to do so, insisting this would keep her group from meeting its goals. Without providing the data to back up this claim or providing any alternative solutions, she quickly moved on to the next subject, leaving the other managers to figure out what to do. Lisa seemed pleased with this outcome, as if protecting her department's turf was her goal rather than working together to accomplish the company's goals.

OBSERVATIONS ON THE CASE

Lisa is acting as if she has a win-lose mentality, as though another team must "lose" in order for her team to "win." If Lisa were using systems thinking, she would see that both departments are part of the bigger organizational system designed to meet the organization's mission, vision, and goals. By extension, she would see that keeping information from her teammates in another department merely hurts the overall organization. It is important to help people be more aware of the frames of reference/biases they carry around and how these impact their choices, their followers, and their organizations.

What Individuals Who Think Like an Ethical Leader Do

Thinking like an ethical leader includes assuming responsibility for honoring laws and for following individual and organizational values. It requires a global view and an awareness of how our daily actions and decisions impact multiple constituents that are part of layered and connected systems. Leaders who do this well:

- Include a broad array of stakeholders when making decisions
- Use systems thinking to see connections and interrelationships
- Consider the long-term consequences of their decisions for multiple constituents
- Stay focused on the long-term vision and mission of the organization
- Use their moral intuition along with a more structured ethical decision-making process
- Think like good local and global citizens
- Believe in mutual benefit and act accordingly

Principle Eleven: Do Good Without Doing Harm

Make a habit of two things: to help; or at least to do no harm.

—Hippocrates

This principle—doing good without doing harm—is at the heart of ethical leadership. Doing good without doing harm requires leaders to ponder how they will know if they are "doing good." Questions to consider include the following:

- How is my leadership affecting the larger society?
- What types of harm could happen as a result of my decisions?
- How can I make sure that my goals are met without doing harm?

Doing Good . . .

Do all the good you can. By all the means you can.
In all the ways you can. In all the places you can.
At all the times you can. To all the people you can.
As long as ever you can.

—John Wesley

Why should we try to do good? "Doing good" represents a high level of moral development and a high degree of concern for others. Leaders who follow the ethical principle of "doing good" make day-to-day decisions for their organizations that improve lives and communities.

The principle of "doing good" is a powerful one that has compounding results and compounding benefits. The companies that "do good" experience benefits from serving others in a meaningful way, including increased employee loyalty, engagement, commitment, and satisfaction, higher levels of customer loyalty, engagement, and retention, and an increased sense of meaning.

Other advantages include higher levels of efficiency in operations, higher levels of perceived product quality, and better financial performance[44] (see Chapter Two for more about the business advantages of ethical leadership).

Think about how your industry and your organization would define "doing good." What would that look like for you? "Doing good" may include doing good for others, the community, society, or the environment, providing a service that improves customers' lives, helping people realize their potential, solving a difficult problem that affects us all, eliminating an element of harm in society, and making the world a better place

The first step in implementing this principle is to be sure that our business goals and the ways in which we do business in fact "do good." Fully understanding "doing good" requires accepting that leadership is fundamentally about relationships and service to others—service to employees, customers, organizations, communities, and society.

Questions for leaders to consider include the following:

- How are we benefiting our customers?

- How are we benefiting our employees?
- How are we benefiting our suppliers?
- How do we leave things better than we found them?
- How are we helping the communities we work in?

It is interesting to note that almost all of the world's religions have "doing good" as one of their tenets. The Socratic concept that doing good is its own reward is reflected in the Old Testament Bible verse, "The kind person benefits himself, but the cruel one harms himself."[45]

. . . Without Doing Harm

Our prime purpose in life is to help others.
And if you can't help them, at least don't hurt them.

—The Dalai Lama

As a result of unethical decisions made without regard for their short- and long-term effect on others, catastrophic changes have occurred in the economy and in the business landscape. In the last few years, we have experienced the fall of major corporations and endured an economic crisis widely blamed on corporate greed.

PREVENTING SOCIETAL HARM

Justice . . . is a kind of compact not to harm or be harmed.

—Epicurus

As leaders, we can't consider our actions and decisions in a vacuum. It's important to remember that we are part of the communities we serve and that we have a responsibility to be a positive influence and to avoid harm. Questions for leaders to consider include these:

- What is the purpose of a business or, in the bigger picture, any economic system?
- What are or should be the goals of the modern corporation?
- What is our social responsibility?

- How do organizations minimize their negative impact on the environment and on society while still making money?

PREVENTING HARM TO LIFE AND ECOSYSTEMS

Ethics, too, are nothing but reverence for life.

—Albert Schweitzer

Laws are designed to prevent harm to life. As a society, we may disagree on the particulars of how to respond to our responsibilities to protect human, plant, and animal life, but ethical leaders believe that life is precious. By Albert Schweitzer's definition, "Reverence for Life is a philosophy that says the only thing we're really sure of is that we live and want to go on living. And this is something that we share with everything else that lives—from elephants to blades of grass."[46] Such a philosophy guides us to protect life in all the ways we can. Schweitzer seemed to understand the complexity and disagreements that would result from this mindset when he said, "Reverence for Life is not some cranky and impossible commandment. It just says we must be aware of what we're doing."[47]

We now realize the scope of the harm that has resulted from years of doing business as if the life and natural resources of our planet were expendable. At this step, the question to ask is, "How am I doing good in ways that avoid doing harm to life, nature, the environment, and ecosystems?"

The sustainability and green movements are powerful; they expect us to consider our negative impact on the natural environment as well as on people and wildlife. Likewise, the concept known as the Precautionary Principle is a good guide for leaders making difficult decisions. As Patrice Sutton explains, "The Precautionary Principle is the idea that action should be taken to prevent harm to the environment and human health, even if scientific evidence is inconclusive."[48]

One way to apply precaution to everyday leadership is to ask, "If the suspicion [that this practice harms] turns out to be true, will I have been leading unethically?"

PREVENTING HARM TO CONSTITUENTS

Perhaps it is impossible for a person who does no good not to do harm.

—Harriet Beecher Stowe

Questions to discuss in assessing how well you are doing in preventing harm to a wide range of constituents include the following:

- In doing what we do, do we know how people are impacted? How will we find out?
- What is the net effect of our work on the natural environment? Are we taking more resources than we put back?
- How do we impact society, including health, safety, intelligence, cooperation, lawfulness, family values, and wellness?
- How could we minimize the harm we do and still succeed?

PRINCIPLE ELEVEN CASE STUDY:
SUPPORTING THE LOCAL FOOD BANK

Christine is a manager who volunteers at the local food bank. She paints in her spare time and is asked to design and make a t-shirt that the food bank can sell to raise money. The funds will be used to buy meat and cheese to stock the refrigerated pantry with high protein foods for hungry families. After Christine's colorful t-shirt design is approved, she begins requesting prices for printing the shirts. She obtains prices and fabric samples from three local printers and chooses one with a location near her office.

When Christine mentions her choice to her friend Rebecca, she is surprised at Rebecca's response. "Didn't you hear about that company being fined for unfair labor practices in its shirt factory overseas?" she asks.

Christine is very thankful that she learned about this ethical problem before she ordered the shirts. After checking out the three printers more thoroughly, she chooses a small printer on the other side of town.

Observations on the Case

In this case, there was an important reason why the regional t-shirt printer could offer such attractive pricing: its shirts were made in an unsafe factory in an impoverished country. Considering shirt price, shirt and printing quality, and the proximity of the printer's shops to her office didn't allow Christine to uncover this issue. Simply put, she left out an important variable to consider when choosing vendors and partners—ethics.

If Christine had chosen the regional printer selling shirts made in unsafe conditions, she would have put the food bank at risk of negative publicity and would have been supporting practices that did not match her values. In the end, she chose to do good (paint a unique design and have it printed on t-shirts the food bank could sell) without doing harm (choosing a t-shirt shop that used ethical practices).

Some business models inherently fail to honor Principle Eleven: Do Good Without Doing Harm. Here are some examples:

- Making illegal drugs that lead to deaths
- Helping other people break the law
- Making legal drugs that do more harm than good
- Providing products and services that are known to increase violence in any way or to otherwise harm people or society
- Using parts or ingredients known or suspected to be harmful in order to increase profitability
- Clear cutting land to keep up with the increasing demand for paper products (or houses or new businesses . . .) or using other unsustainable practices that harm the environment

Honoring principle eleven requires honoring both sides of an important equation—doing good and doing it in a way that does not harm.

What Leaders Who Do Good Without Doing Harm Do

Leaders who do good without doing harm keep up with changes in the world. They take the time to consider multiple variables and constituents when making decisions. They check ethical track records before choosing partners and vendors.

Doing good without doing harm is a high-level responsibility that is only achievable when we are morally aware (principle two), stay competent (principle three), respect others (principle five) and think like an ethical leader (principle ten). Leaders who do good in ways that do not harm are creating a net benefit to society and leaving a legacy that makes a positive difference. Such leaders:

- See their role as one of service to others
- Actively prevent harm to people and the planet
- Create products and services that solve problems and do not harm
- Choose ethical partners and suppliers who apply the principles in this book
- Contribute to the betterment of society
- Use recycled or repurposed materials to protect land and natural resources
- Avoid polluting or altering the environment in ways that harm life or ecosystems
- Avoid using parts or ingredients or processes that are known or suspected to be harmful
- See themselves as responsible for leaving things better than they found them
- Promote non-violent solutions to problems

Principle 12: Work for Mutually Beneficial Solutions

We can really respect a man only if he doesn't always look out for himself.

—Johann Wolfgang von Goethe

The goal of an ethical leader is to lead collaboratively, bringing out the best in everyone and seeking win-win solutions to problems. However, certain barriers must be addressed before a company can consistently work toward mutually beneficial solutions at all levels.

Profit As the Only Goal

Rabindra Kanungo and Manuel Mendonca write in *Ethical Dimensions of Leadership*, "Even unethical means seem to be justified in the relentless pursuit of profit."[49] As discussed in Chapter Three, using profit as the only lens for decision making is a major problem, and wanting profits to be the most important thing doesn't make it so.

Profitability can be an outcome when an organization uses good business practices based on responsible corporate citizenship and when other aspects of good leadership are practiced. When an organization creates a culture in which profitability is a goal in and of itself, though, decisions may shortchange other important short- and long-term factors and lead the organization to ethical failure.

If a company can make more money by ignoring its impact on its customers, then it is winning at their expense. Think about a global company selling products containing potentially harmful ingredients to U.S. consumers because current regulations do not prevent it, while offering safer alternatives in other countries that have tighter regulations. If a safer alternative is available, why only offer it to *some* consumers? Honoring human rights requires us to treat all people with care.

Win-Lose Thinking

Win-lose thinking is the desire to win, even if it means that someone else loses in ways that may harm them. In the example of the global company I just mentioned, using win-lose thinking might lead us to think that it is acceptable to delay offering a safer alternative until laws specifically require it.

A win-win thinker, by contrast, might think about how to make a profit while taking care to consider the impact of decisions and products on *all* customers. That thinking might include considering the positive consumer response to precaution, the likelihood that laws will soon change, and the market benefits of using safer ingredients before competitors do so. A win-win thinker would want to offer mutual benefit and avoid harm to others.

A Scarcity Mentality

A person using a scarcity mentality believes there is not enough to go around. The perception may be that there are not enough customers, not enough materials, not enough land, or not enough of some other important component of the leader's business model. When we believe there is not enough to go around, we usually believe that in order to succeed, we have to take something away from somebody else. This way of thinking could be characterized at the leader and organization level as similar to the "fight or flight" reaction of an individual facing a situation of great danger.

The scarcity way of thinking is confrontational and compartmentalized. It leads to treating the interests of different parties as if they were mutually exclusive. In this way of thinking, "There isn't enough for both of us, so I have to get it before you do."

This "us against them" thinking rarely considers that there very well could be a solution that would make us all happy. It rarely considers interrelationships and the cyclical nature of work and systems. Instead, it usually leads to narrow, short-term thinking and poor decisions.

Inability to Handle Complexity

While the scarcity way of thinking is confrontational and compartmentalized, an inability to handle complexity effectively can also lead to oversimplified solutions to complex problems and a failure to achieve mutually beneficial solutions.

Imagine needing to make a decision and being overwhelmed by conflicting opinions. It is tempting to make a quick choice instead of looking through all the feedback for common themes and considering the impact on multiple constituents. Making a quick choice often leaves out stakeholders that should have been considered, violating the principle of mutual benefit. When we use quick, oversimplified thinking, we seldom end up with an ethical solution to a complex problem.

Ethical leaders embrace the chaos and complexity of the changing workplace and the changing nature of leadership and society. They see complexity as part of life and grapple with the difficult questions about when simplifying things will help and when working within a higher degree of complexity will benefit multiple stakeholders in the long run.

Building Mutually Beneficial Solutions

Mutual benefit is an important aspect of ethical leadership. When we work toward it, we demonstrate an ability to think beyond ourselves, we show respect and care for others, and we create mutual value.

Ethical leaders work to build mutually beneficial solutions no matter how many stakeholders there are. Such leaders first learn what each party's goals are, agree on how to work together and make decisions, and seek solutions that honor the goals of all parties in mutually beneficial ways. It takes some creativity to come up with solutions that honor multiple goals, but it is well worth the effort, because mutually beneficial agreements and partnerships last.

PRINCIPLE 12 CASE STUDY:
DEVELOPER DILEMMA

Michael runs a construction company that builds condos for developers. Sales have been slow recently and he is getting pressure from the developers to use cheaper parts to increase their profits on future builds. Michael suspects that the cheaper parts they want him to use will fail quickly and will be costly for condo owners to replace.

Wanting to protect his reputation as a quality builder who doesn't cut corners, Michael spends part of a weekend researching reliable alternatives. He finds a company that offers an alternative with a durability warranty, and it costs less than the product he has been using. Michael contacts the owner and checks out the company's reputation. When everything looks good, he places an order.

To communicate what he learned to the developers, Michael creates a product board and mounts three samples on it—the quality product he had been using, the flimsy one they wanted him to use, and the alternative he found. Seeing how flimsy the part was that they had initially requested, the developers thanked Michael for taking the initiative to find a less expensive replacement that was better quality.

OBSERVATIONS ON THE CASE

Michael could have folded under the pressure the developers placed on him to meet their profit needs. Doing that, though, would have been unethical and would have violated his principles. He realized that the condo owners were silent stakeholders, and their needs had to be considered. He did not want them to have to deal with unplanned repairs, and there was always a chance of safety problems if parts failed at key points that affected structural integrity.

Instead of using the parts chosen by the developers or refusing to use them, Michael sought a solution that would benefit him, the developers, and the condo owners. Finding mutually beneficial solutions to day-to-day problems demonstrates care and concern for others in tangible ways. By taking the time to find a mutually beneficial alternative, he built credibility with the developers and protected his reputation as a quality builder.

What Leaders Who Seek Mutually Beneficial Solutions Do
While less ethical leaders might get as much they can while giving as little as possible or take unfair advantage of others, leaders who seek mutually beneficial solutions work to benefit all parties involved. They think broadly and long-term and take the time to reach a positive solution that is a mutual win. They respect the needs of silent stakeholders, like the condo owners in the case study, who cannot speak for themselves but who are affected by the outcome. They intentionally:

- Think beyond their own gain and consider the needs of others
- Make sure agreements are fair and beneficial to all parties
- Seek creative alternatives that meet the needs of all stakeholders
- Find out what each party wants and work together on how to accomplish these goals using shared resources
- Use creativity and open communication to find mutually beneficial alternatives
- Protect silent stakeholders who are affected by the outcome

Together, principles ten, eleven, and twelve focus on how to Lead With Positive Intent and Impact. In Chapter Seven, I explore how to Lead For the Greater Good and introduce the two final principles that, together, represent the highest level of ethical leadership.

7

Lead for the Greater Good

*Man can "look before and after." He can transcend the immediate
moment, can remember the past and plan for the future, and thus
choose a good which is greater, but will not occur till some
future moment in preference to a lesser, immediate one.*

—Rollo May

14 Guiding Principles of Ethical Leadership

Lead With a Moral Compass

1. Demonstrate Personal Congruence
2. Be Morally Aware
3. Stay Competent
4. Model Expected Performance and Leadership

Lead in Ways That Bring Out the Best in Others

5. Respect Others
6. Respect Boundaries
7. Trust and Be Trustworthy
8. Communicate Openly
9. Generate Effective and Ethical Performance

Lead For the Greater Good

13. Protect Our Planet for Future Generations
14. Improve Our Global Society for Future Generations

Lead With Positive Intent and Impact

10. Think Like an Ethical Leader
11. Do Good Without Doing Harm
12. Work for Mutually Beneficial Solutions

W e share a planet that moves through space at thousands of miles per hour.[50] We share common struggles and milestones regardless of gender, nationality, or race. As George Washington Carver once said, "How far you go in life depends on your being tender with the young, compassionate with the aged, sympathetic with the striving, and tolerant of the weak and strong. Because someday in life you will have been all of these."[51]

Leaving things better than we found them includes honoring the global environment we depend on for survival. It includes improving lives and communities and making choices that are ethical, global, and for the long term.

Principle Thirteen: Protect Our Planet for Future Generations

A civilization flourishes when people plant trees under which they will never sit.

—Greek proverb

Initial questions to ask ourselves about protecting our planet for future generations include "How am I protecting natural life and ecosystems?" and "How am I leaving the planet better than I found it?"

Ecological responsibility is a complex issue, and thoughtful people disagree on how far to go. We are seeing the effects of years of doing business as if the natural resources of our planet were expendable, including an increasing number of extinctions and a reduction in plant and animal diversity. Margaret Wheatley said, "Probably the most visible example of unintended consequences, is what happens every time humans try to change the natural ecology of a place."[52]

Honoring principle thirteen involves asking additional hard questions like, "What will the combined impact of the work we are doing now on the planet over the next five hundred years be?" and "How many natural resources will we take, how much waste will we return, and what will the net effect be?" Knowing the answers to these questions helps us talk about what we can change that will still lead to profitability and customer satisfaction while preventing short- and long-term harm to the environment.

As business leaders, demonstrating care for the planet demonstrates reverence for life. Due to limited natural resources and growing demand for them, it is also critical for our own future success. One way that we can demonstrate care for the planet as we make decisions is by using the concept I introduced earlier called the Precautionary Principle.

Using Precaution in Decision Making

> *A responsible business protects and, where possible, improves the environment, and avoids wasteful use of resources. A responsible business ensures that its operations comply with best environmental management practices consistent with meeting the needs of today without compromising the needs of future generations.*

—Caux Roundtable Principles for Responsible Business

The Precautionary Principle is a good guide for leaders who are making difficult decisions about their impact on the planet. Philippe Grandjean explains that "The precautionary principle (PP) is an extension of the public health approach that prevention is better than cure."[53]

Following the Precautionary Principle means that we avoid using product ingredients that are or *might be* harmful to life and ecosystems. Using this principle, we do much more than simply follow the law (the punishment threshold). Rather, we make the decision that is in the best long-term interests of the planet and natural life. It is not surprising that the Precautionary Principle is gaining momentum as the way to best deal with risk and human and environmental safety.

As we learn more about our impact on the planet and how that impact threatens our shared future, we need to act with care. Looking at ethics on a global scale and our world as one global community, it makes sense to err on the side of caution when evaluating the possible harm our choices could cause.

Meeting Sustainable Business Expectations

*Earth provides enough to satisfy every
man's need, but not every man's greed.*

—Mahatma Gandhi

Ethical leaders must grapple with tough questions like the following as
they respond to the expectation that they do business sustainably:

- How can we protect the environment while making our products
  and still make a profit?
- What is the net effect of our work on the natural environment?
  Are we taking more resources than we put back?
- How do we impact the natural systems needed to support life,
  including the water cycle, plant and animal reproduction, marine
  life, pollination for future food supply, biodiversity, and air
  quality?
- What would happen to the environment if we kept working the
  same way we are now for a hundred more years?
- How can we accomplish our work in ways that still meet our
  goals while protecting natural life and the planet?

Sustainable business practices include paying attention to big and small
choices like energy use, use of raw materials, and the overall footprint of a
business. Ernst and Young observes an increasing awareness about sustainable business, reporting that "A significant number of survey respondents
said they are being asked by key constituencies about sustainable sourcing
and procurement of raw materials."[54]

Tilde Hererra writes, "The concept of sustainability is increasingly
seen as a need-to-have by corporate boards and CEOs, rather than a nice-
to-have. Sustainability carries with it a range of quantifiable, bottom-line
benefits that enhance competitiveness, such as resource efficiency."[55]

In the next one hundred years, we will be improving processes across
sectors and industries. We will be learning how to make food production
and transportation more sustainable while at the same time working to
fix pollution problems that are compounding. Leaders who proactively

work for improvements in the sustainability of their businesses will be ready to respond to rapidly increasing expectations.

PRINCIPLE THIRTEEN CASE STUDY: HOLDING SUPPLIERS ACCOUNTABLE

Philip, the CEO of a paper company, has been carefully monitoring consumer expectations for ethics and environmental best practices over the last few months. After initiating a thorough review of his company's impact on the environment, paying special attention to sustainable sourcing of materials throughout the supply chain, he is disappointed to find that he cannot easily determine the ethics of some of his company's current suppliers. Some of them don't have ethics policies, and others don't want to share this information.

Philip makes a difficult decision that he knows will be best in the long run. He gives his suppliers thirty days to demonstrate that they use ethical practices and sustainable sourcing. If they fail to meet the deadline, he tells them, they will be replaced. Two suppliers fail to meet the deadline and are replaced.

Four months later, Philip's biggest competitor is featured on the front page of a major news magazine with the headline "Global Paper Company Using Supplier Fined for Clear-cutting." Philip realizes what a close call this is, since his company used the same vendor until very recently. He vows to watch all the parts of his supply chain more closely in the future, and to that end he initiates regular reviews and site inspections.

OBSERVATIONS ON THE CASE

In this case, Philip kept up with trends, best practices, and consumer sentiment about ethics, which honored both Principle Two: Be Morally Aware and Principle Three: Stay Competent. Since his suppliers harvest trees, when he decided to hold them accountable for using sustainable practices, he honored Principle Thirteen: Protect Our Planet for Future Generations. That decision also helped him avoid the negative publicity

continues ▶

that a competitor is now dealing with, which gives his company an edge in the marketplace.

Leading for a sustainable future requires thinking beyond individual gain and making tough decisions that are in the best long-term interests of the planet. To do that, we must think of the planet as a silent stakeholder in decision-making. Approaches that fail to do that, and do not honor Principle Thirteen: Protect Our Planet for Future Generations include:

- Lobbying for the right to use ingredients that are known to harm or are suspected of harming the planet, life, or ecosystems
- Polluting air, water, or land
- Clear-cutting land to increase profits, leaving the ecosystem devastated

What Leaders Who Protect Our Planet for Future Generations Do

Leaders who protect our planet for future generations realize that we all must share limited resources wisely. They think about how their practices impact natural life and ecosystems, use sustainable practices, and act to avoid harm. More specifically, they:

- Think long-term
- Treat nature, the environment, and life with care
- Think of the planet as a silent stakeholder when making decisions
- Use precaution in protecting ecosystems and resources
- Reduce, reuse, and recycle waste
- Use sustainably harvested materials
- Repurpose or recycle outdated equipment and raw materials
- Limit energy and water use with automatic water faucets and light switches
- Work toward a zero footprint (no negative impact on the planet)

Principle Fourteen: Improve Our Global Society for Future Generations

The ultimate test of a moral society is the kind of world that it leaves to its children.

—Dietrich Bonhoeffer

The definition of ethical leadership is changing to reflect what we have learned the hard way as a society. Leaders now have to keep up with a complex array of evolving standards that represent responsible business in today's workplace. Being part of a global marketplace means that we must consider the long-term international impact of business decisions.

Embracing the Global Greater Good

It is the greatest good to the greatest number of people which is the measure of right and wrong.

—Jeremy Bentham

In Chapter Three, I described the greater good as leadership that is greater than ourselves, greater than our own interests, greater than our own works, and greater than our own lifetimes. Considering the greater good is the broadest perspective of ethical leadership.

Considering the greater good in business life includes the difficult challenges of:

- Considering complex problems carefully
- Using a systems perspective to see the interrelationships between natural and man-made systems
- Considering multiple perspectives and emerging information (not just data confirming a business's current direction)
- Making decisions that do no harm
- Providing services and products that benefit the greater good of society

107

Our approach to economic freedom has led to a wide variety of choices for consumers, some of them good and some of them not so good for society. The new consumer is much better informed and is no longer drawn to what is "not so good." Businesses providing services and products that do harm, or that do not seem to benefit society in any way, will feel the impact of higher consumer expectations in the coming years.

Consumers are more frequently making the connection between their purchasing choices and the state of our economic and social well-being. They now expect business leaders to make that connection and to make wise choices that consider long-term impacts on communities, the environment, and society. Remi Trudel and June Cotte of the University of Western Ontario researched whether or not consumers would pay more for ethically produced goods. They found that customers will pay a premium for ethically produced goods and also demand lower prices from companies not seen as ethical.[56]

Consumers are increasingly concerned about the impact of products and services on their health, the environment, and natural resources. Employees are increasingly concerned about working for companies that lead ethically in a wide variety of contexts.

Ethical leadership guidelines cross disciplines and geographic boundaries and have been adopted by diverse groups of world leaders. Such global benchmarks include the UN Global Compact, the Caux Roundtable Principles for Responsible Business, and the Global Economic Ethic: Consequences for Global Business. These guidelines provide an easy way for business leaders who are ready to embrace the new broader "ethical leadership" to know how to respond.

Care for Global Society Over the Long Term

If we could but recognize our common humanity, that we do belong together, that our destinies are bound up in one another's, that we can be free only together, that we can survive only together, that we can be human only together . . .

—Desmond Tutu, South African bishop and civil rights activist

Businesses that support communities and the "social good" of society are being recognized in the media as leaders and are gaining powerful reputation capital. Leading this way adds to the brand value of these businesses. Indeed, Ethical Brand Value, or EBV, is now being discussed as an important part of corporate branding.

Ethical leaders generate value well beyond the company walls, adding value for constituents while making a profit responsibly. Customers, shareholders, investors, employees, communities, and suppliers benefit when businesses work to ensure a better future. As leaders, we can't consider our actions and decisions in a vacuum. We are part of the communities we serve, and we have a responsibility to be a positive influence (do good) and avoid harm. Questions like those that follow help us consider how well we are improving global society for future generations:

- How do we consider our impact on future generations when making decisions?
- In doing what we do, what is our effect, positive and negative, on our global society?
- How do we positively impact health, safety, cooperation, lawfulness, and wellness?

Principle Fourteen Case Study:
In the Long Run

Brook is the owner of a large auto dealership that is growing, and wants to expand. For a year, she has been trying to buy the parcel of land on both sides of her dealership so that she can add a larger waiting room, more service bays, and additional parking.

A real estate attorney is helping Brook in her attempts to purchase the land. After investigating, the attorney reports that there are already plans in the works for the land on both sides of the dealership, and in fact, the city wants to buy out the dealership's property in order to build a new hospital on the site. The planned hospital would feature specialized care and equipment that is not currently available in this part of the country.

Brook is stunned by this news. She has invested a great deal of time and money in the dealership and is ready to expand. Now she has to choose between staying in cramped quarters or building on a new site. She discusses the news with her top managers and hears a wide range of concerns and ideas from them. They talk about how moving would let them reconfigure the space, which would be an advantage, but changing the address and marketing materials and retaining customers who are used to going to the old location would be hard for the dealership to manage, given its current staffing.

After sleeping on it, Brook decides to use a book she's read recently to help her make the most responsible decision. She evaluates her options using the 7 Lenses and 14 Guiding Principles, and when she's finished, she calls a meeting of her managers to discuss what she plans to do.

Here are Brook's notes:

Looking at the Options through the 7 Lenses

Option 1 (Sell)	Option 2 (Stay)
(Lens One) **The Profit Lens**	We can make a profit either way. If we are paid a fair price for the dealership when we sell, we can build a more efficiently designed one with room for expansion. I wonder if we will find enough land close enough to this location that we can keep our current customers.
(Lens Two) **The Law Lens**	Both options are legal. I wonder if the city has the power to make us leave if we decide not to sell.
(Lens Three) **The Character Lens**	Blocking the building of a new hospital doesn't seem like it demonstrates good character. On the other hand, the way I've been running the dealership, I have shown good character over the years. This new situation changes the rules.
(Lens Four) **The People Lens**	Employees and customers could be inconvenienced by the move if we sell. Citizens would be inconvenienced or harmed if the specialized medical care isn't available.

continues ▶

(Lens Five) **The Communities Lens**	People would clearly benefit from the new hospital if we sell to make way for it. It will save lives. They will benefit from the dealership wherever we locate it.
(Lens Six) **The Planet Lens**	Building a more energy efficient dealership on a new site would save energy and water. Could we get a grant to help us build the first solar powered dealership in the state?
(Lens Seven) **The Greater Good Lens**	The hospital is needed, and is for the long-term good of the region. Meanwhile, we are running out of space. If we can find suitable land, moving would help us deal with our space problems and improve our energy efficiency at the same time. If we can get enough money for the land and find funding toward building an energy efficient dealership, we can make this work toward everyone's future good.

LOOKING AT THE OPTIONS IN TERMS OF THE 14 GUIDING PRINCIPLES

Lead With a Moral Compass

While they won't all be happy about moving, I think our employees will be upset if I block the building of the new hospital by refusing to sell. I have been committed to building a strong community and they know that, so selling the land will demonstrate personal congruence and moral awareness.

Lead in Ways That Bring Out the Best in Others

I will need to openly explain the pros and cons of this move so that people will know I have thought it through carefully and considered their needs.

While a move will be disruptive, I think we can generate more effective performance in a well-designed space.

Lead With Positive Intent and Impact

The more I think about it, the more I like the mutually beneficial solution of moving to make way for the new hospital while building a state-of-the-art energy-efficient facility that others can use as a model. It's a bit risky, but it will position us much better for the future.

Lead for the Greater Good

Selling the land and opening a new dealership will require a lot of work, but in the long run it will be in the best interests of this business and society.

We're going to need an architect and a builder with experience in projects of this type. We'll need them to "think green" and be aware of the conservation laws and best practices involved in building auto dealerships.

It's time to look for suitable land and figure out the finances of this decision.

OBSERVATIONS ON THE CASE

Brook was not able to pursue her plans for expansion, but she found a mutually beneficial alternative that may be better for her business in the long run. She had to quickly adapt to new information that changed the ethics of her decision while letting go of her deeply held expansion mindset. As she did that, she began to see the possibilities. While the details are not yet worked out, Brook is motivated to move forward with a plan that is a win for all parties.

In her decision-making, Brook considered which choice would show the most congruence with her values. She involved her team in the process and considered the impact that the move would have on them. She weighed the impact on the community, the greater good, and on

continues ▶

her long-term profitability. This kind of broad thinking that considers multiple stakeholders is what ethical leadership is all about. We can use this kind of thinking in our day-to-day decisions too, not just the big ones like the one Brook had to make.

What Leaders Who Improve Our
Global Society for Future Generations Do

Leaders who honor this principle of ethical leadership think beyond themselves not just for their lifetimes but for the lifetimes of future generations. They honor the concept of "leaving things better than we found them" and strive to make the world a better place through their leadership choices. Leaders honoring this principle:

- Think hundreds of years into the future when making decisions
- Treat people, communities, nature, the environment, and life with care
- Balance their own interests with the good of society
- Broadly do good and avoid harm
- Use a precautionary approach
- Contribute to the global good, leaving the world better than they found it

Together, the 7 Lenses and 14 Guiding Principles represent ethical leadership in a complex world. These lenses and principles are connected and interdependent, operating as a system. Focusing too much on any one component in isolation can lead to the neglect of ethics in another. Applying *all* of these perspectives to our work using a kaleidoscopic view increases the chances that we will make ethical decisions. The quick summary that concludes this chapter can be used as a checklist for making decisions that honor all 7 Lenses and all 14 Guiding Principles.

With this foundational view of ethical leadership established, I turn my attention in the final chapter to where ethical leadership is headed, to the six connected trends I see shaping the future of ethical leadership, and to how ethical leaders can be ready for what lies ahead.

Quick Summary of the 7 Lenses and Their Accompanying Responsibilities

Lens:	Responsibilities:
Profit	____ Long-term business success
	____ Profiting responsibly
Law	____ Laws, regulations, and guidelines
	____ Focus on ethical values, not just following laws
Character	____ Integrity, honesty and personal congruence
	____ Competence, moral awareness and openness to learning
	____ Modeling good performance and leadership
People	____ Care, human rights and full inclusion
	____ Respect for others, differences and boundaries
	____ Trust and trustworthiness
	____ Open communication
	____ Generating effective and ethical performance
Communities	____ Service, giving back in ways that improve lives and communities
	____ Doing good without doing harm
	____ Working for mutually beneficial solutions
Planet	____ Respect for life, nature, and ecosystems
	____ Sustainable business practices, systems thinking, precaution
	____ Treating the planet as a silent stakeholder
Greater Good	____ Using long-term ethical thinking
	____ Improving global society and the quality of life for future generations

Part 3

How Are Ethical
Expectations Changing?

We now have 7 Lenses through which to view our ethical responsibilities as leaders and 14 Guiding Principles for honoring constituents and making ethical choices. These 7 Lenses and 14 Guiding Principles help us understand and fulfill our ethical responsibilities as leaders. To be prepared for the future, however, we also need to understand the broader trends that are raising ethical expectations. Understanding ethical leadership trends and why they are happening helps us aim for where ethical leadership will be in the future and gives us a broad awareness of what it means to lead ethically for the long term.

Think about some ethical standards that have already been raised during your lifetime. These may include minimum fuel efficiency and maximum emissions allowed in newly manufactured cars, granting additional rights to groups of people, or preventing bullying or harassment in the workplace. In Part Three, I will explore the common threads that connect these changes and how they are raising overall expectations for ethical leadership.

8

Getting Ready for the Future of Ethical Leadership

We have learned that growth, profitability and meeting goals are worthy causes only when undertaken in the context of responsible business practices. The laws are changing, but even more important, there is a powerful movement toward more ethical leadership, and it is gaining momentum.

—Linda Fisher Thornton

Our understanding of ethical leadership is continually evolving due to changes in the world and to the efforts of champions of responsible business. This evolving understanding incorporates the natural complexity of the challenges of leadership and the broadening scope of the constituents that leaders serve. As we move from thinking about leadership as "transactional" to thinking about leadership for the "greater good," we increase our understanding of our moral responsibilities to others, our companies, our societies, and our world.

How Leadership Evolves From
"Transactions" to the "Greater Good"

The graphic that follows shows how our collective understanding of the purpose of leadership has shifted in important ways that parallel human moral development as described in Chapter Three. Leadership was once considered transactional, without much of a human element in it at all. This one-way mindset was essentially based on "Tell people what you need them to do." Fortunately, the general thinking about leadership shifted to include a service role, which brought the all-important human element into it. Later, we began to understood leadership as having a positive and transformative effect on individuals, groups, and organizations. In this evolution, leadership had moved from being about self to considering self and others.

After incorporating others in our understanding of leadership, we began to add a consideration of society. Through the Corporate Social Responsibility movement, leadership responsibilities are now seen to include sustainability and community well-being. We are currently experiencing a powerful leadership movement to support the greater good of society, representing the kind of leadership that works for all of humanity. This is ethical leadership at its highest level, on a global scale.

The Evolving Purpose of Leadership:
From Transactions to the Greater Good

These changes in our understanding of the purpose of leadership have happened slowly over time. Understanding them helps us stay ahead of the curve, to be better prepared to lead in ways that meet future expectations. In this chapter, I explore six connected trends in ethical leadership that offer a sense of where this field is headed. Aiming for where ethical leadership will be in the future will help us move from a chaotic uncertainty about how to lead ethically to a clarity about what we need to focus on and do.

I see six connected trends shaping the future of ethical leadership. These include:

1. Broadening scope
2. Increased visibility
3. Focus on protecting human rights
4. Companies contributing to society
5. Managing ethics as a performance system
6. Retooling skills to stay ethically competent

Understanding these six trends will help us stay ethically aware in a fast-changing global society. Looking at these six trends together illuminates why we are seeing frequent changes in laws and hints at areas in which we can expect to see more changes.

1. Broadening Scope

Our conception of the corporate sphere of influence will therefore widen to include yet more issues of public good and even more distant stages of the value chain.

−Andrew Crane, York University, Toronto

The increasingly broad scope of ethical leadership can make training leaders on ethical leadership seem a bit overwhelming. The scope of our topic is expanding rapidly, making it difficult to know where to draw the line. Some of the factors contributing to the wider scope of what we call "ethical leadership" are shown on the next page.

Elements of the Broadening Scope of Ethical Leadership	How Our Thinking Needs to Change
Beyond the local mindset to the global mindset	We need to expand our thinking from within the radius of a city or a state or country to thinking like global citizens.
From short-term thinking to long-term thinking	We need to expand our thinking from this quarter's profits to our impact on the community and the environment for generations.
Beyond diversity and inclusion to full inclusion	We can think beyond the types of diverse populations within our organization to focus on full inclusion.[57]
Considering multiple stakeholders	In a globally connected society, leadership is more collective and a business's impact is greater. Stakeholders to consider used to include customers, employees, managers, shareholders, and the community. Now they also include the environment, suppliers, future generations, society, and competitors (who may become partners). In essence, "everyone" could be our stakeholder.
Including multifaceted business responsibilities	We don't just need to think about ethics when we realize we're making an ethical decision; we need to consider the ethics of everything we do in every context.
Thinking across disciplines to solve complex problems	Disciplines are ways of looking at the world. Looking at ethics (or any other aspect of leadership) across disciplines provides a much clearer picture. Thinking and researching across disciplines is becoming a necessary skill as problems become increasingly complex. A view from within any one discipline can be too narrow to provide a clear solution. Looking beyond the boundaries that define a discipline can help us solve tough problems.

2. Increased Visibility

> *It is, indeed, an age of information where there are no secrets and there's no place to hide anymore.*

–Keith Darcy, Ethics and Compliance Officer Association

Our leaders and their choices are visible, and the public is openly talking about them. What we do defines our brands, and as consumers increasingly want to support ethical brands in a volatile global economy, our choices impact our profitability and organizational viability. The increased visibility of ethical leadership has made it a central component of brand value. For meaning-seeking employees, as illustrated below, it has become a critical factor in employment decisions.

Elements of the Increased Visibility of Ethical Leadership	How Our Thinking Needs to Change
Ethical consumerism	We need to evaluate and improve the ethics of every product and service we offer. Customers are increasingly choosing products based on ethics and their desire to support ethical businesses. They have ethical shopping apps to guide their purchasing decisions.
Online reviews	We need to focus on providing a positive experience that honors ethical principles. Consumers share their experiences with the world, and we need to make sure we are providing good experiences fueled by good ethics and good leadership.
Savvy job-seekers	We need to build respectful, high-trust organizations and make ethical leadership a priority. Employees are increasingly seeking meaningful work, respectful workplaces, and ethical leaders. Our proactive ethical leadership will impact important business metrics that include recruitment, retention, and employee engagement.

continues ▶

Elements of the Increased Visibility of Ethical Leadership, con't.	How Our Thinking Needs to Change, con't.
Ethical violations widely covered in the news	We need to intentionally manage our ethical leadership in ways that put us in the news for doing good, not for harming or exploiting.
Ethics as part of brand value	We need to intentionally manage ethical leadership as part of the organizational brand management strategy.

3. Focus on Protecting Human Rights

It is relatively easy for an enterprise to say that it respects human rights—and it may do so in the genuine belief that that is the case. But to make that claim with legitimacy, an enterprise needs both to know and to be able to show that it is indeed respecting human rights in practice.

—United Nations Human Rights, Office of the High Commissioner for Human Rights, *The Corporate Responsibility to Respect Human Rights: An Interpretive Guide*

How we interpret and respond to human rights will determine the kind of experience that people have in our organizations. There is a growing awareness that despite our variety and differences, we are all part of one humanity. As such, we are required to treat each other with a high degree of respect and care. Proactive companies, as described below, are posting detailed Human Rights Policy statements on their websites to inform customers and prospective employees of their commitment to honoring human rights.

Elements of the Focus on Protecting Human Rights	How Our Thinking Needs to Change
Growing human rights awareness	We need to acknowledge that we are each unique and all connected. We are dependent on one another for survival in a rapidly changing world with limited space and resources.
The Universal Declaration of Human Rights	We need to honor universal human values. There is a strong movement toward honoring universal values that are created by diverse groups of global leaders. These values reflect honoring the rights and dignity of each person in many important ways.
Harm is being interpreted more broadly	We need to prevent negative stress. Prolonged stress has been proven to damage the brain and contribute to disease. Because we are now aware of this, "harm" is expanded to include unethical interpersonal behaviors like verbal abuse, belittling, and bullying.
Care is an important aspect of ethical leadership	We need to demonstrate care. Because of increased awareness of human rights, care is becoming a major issue in ethical leadership.
Respect is the "minimum standard" for workplace behavior	We need to expect respectful behavior. Employee expectations, consumer expectations, and market expectations of ethical leadership include using respectful behavior.
To respond to a new awareness about human rights, companies are posting human rights policy statements	We need to proactively support human rights. Companies are declaring their awareness of human rights and their commitment to support them.

4. Companies Contributing to Society

The self-interested pursuit of profit, with no concern for other stakeholders, will ultimately lead to business failure and, at times, to counterproductive regulation. Consequently, business leaders must always assert ethical leadership so as to protect the foundations of sustainable prosperity.

—Caux Roundtable Principles for Responsible Business

Our global understanding of the purpose of business has evolved. It's not enough any more just to make money responsibly. As detailed below, businesses are understood to have a clear responsibility to society, and that responsibility is not just for today. It must include the generations to come.[58]

Elements of Companies Contributing to Society	How Our Thinking Needs to Change
Considering business impact on others and society	We need to teach organizational leaders how to use intentional ethical thinking, provide the opportunity to practice ethical thinking, and talk openly about the impact of the business on multiple constituents.
Considering business impact on the environment	We need to find ways to honor Principle Thirteen: Protect Our Planet for Future Generations and still meet organizational goals. There are more affordable options available every year.
Considering unintended consequences of actions	We need to use systems thinking and the Precautionary Principle and to carefully consider the 7 Lenses and 14 Guiding Principles when making decisions.
Improving lives and communities	We need to participate in community service in ways that transform the community and bring out the best in those who participate.
Making a difference in the world	We need to make leading for the greater good part of our ethical leadership agenda.

5. Managing Ethics As a System

Don't just talk about ethics. Make it an integral part
of the fabric of your company and the way you do business.

—2012 National Business Ethics Survey® of Fortune 500®
Employees, Ethics Resource Center

When we manage ethics as a program, we deliver it, keep records about who attended, and move on. Managing ethics as a system requires that we take an integrated and aligned approach to managing ethics.

As highlighted below, organizations that manage ethical leadership as a system and generate an ongoing dialogue will find that they are more likely to get the behavior they expect and that employees will feel a sense of shared ownership in managing ethics throughout the organization.

Elements of Managing Ethics As a System	How Our Thinking Needs to Change
Communicate clear ethical leadership expectations and have an ethics code	We need to move from vague statements of leadership values to specific ethical expectations that are clear to all leaders.
Make those expectations an integrated component of all performance management systems	We need to build our ethical leadership performance management system around the expectations and align all people practices with them.
Make ethics an integral part of all leadership development	We need to weave ethical leadership throughout all leadership development rather than teaching it as a separate subject, which can create the impression that it is separate from day-to-day leadership.
Hold leaders at all levels accountable for ethical interpersonal behavior and ethical leadership	We need to make no exceptions based on status or position. We need to hold leaders at all levels accountable.
Align all elements of performance management with ethical leadership expectations	We need to align all performance management practices including performance feedback, reviews, and rewards with these ethical leadership expectations.

continues ▶

Elements of Managing Ethics As a System, con't.	How Our Thinking Needs to Change , con't.
Generate ongoing, open communication about ethical values, ethical decision-making, and ethical behavior	We need to generate an open, ongoing dialogue, making it safe for people to ask questions and talk about difficult ethical issues.
Provide opportunities for people to practice identifying ethical issues and making ethical decisions	We need to build practice into manager meetings and ongoing training programs.
Notice and reward ethical choices and behavior	We need to make ethics a priority when distributing recognition and rewards.
Share what can be learned from ethical failures in your company and industry	We need to approach ethical leadership from a proactive learning perspective, with the intent of getting better every day.

6. Retooling Skills to Stay Ethically Competent

The skill sets required have changed—more complex thinkers [are] needed. Reflecting the changes in the environment, the competencies that will be most valuable to the future leader appear to be changing.

—Nick Petrie, Center for Creative Leadership

The sixth trend is the continual need to retool our skills due to a high degree of work complexity and the need to stay ethically aware and competent as times change. While organizations are increasingly providing ethical leadership development for their leaders, many leaders are also taking their development into their own hands.

As the world changes, we must constantly stretch to respond with new leadership skills and abilities. During slow times in business due to the economy or other factors, proactive leaders build the skills they will need when business picks up.

The IBM 2012 Global CEO Study reported that "companies that outperform their peers are thirty percent more likely to identify openness—often characterized by a greater use of social media as a key enabler of collaboration and innovation—as a key influence in their organization."[59]

The same study reported that CEOs rank collaboration, communication, creativity, and flexibility as central to employee behavior in a more interconnected environment. Other factors involved in retooling our skills to stay ethically competent are laid out below.

Elements of Retooling Skills to Stay Ethically Competent	How Our Thinking Needs to Change
Global awareness	We need to be thinking as global citizens, learning to share control and collaborate across boundaries with multiple stakeholders that sometimes have conflicting goals.
Ethical competence	We need to continually sharpen our ethical awareness and improve our ethical competence.
Ethical behavior and choices	We need to carefully and intentionally think about the ethics of our behavior. We should consider the ethical implications of every decision.
Learning to handle complexity	We need to use creativity and innovation and be comfortable not having "the right answer." We're dealing with complex processes, and the answers depend on how we view the problem.
Embracing social media	We need to use social media for learning and communication. We're a networked, globally connected world. Customers and prospects as well as employees and future employees are looking for our responsible consistent presence on social media.
Systematically building ethical leadership skills over time	We need to approach leadership as a lifelong learning journey and make noticeable progress over time in our ethical awareness and the ethics of our behavior and decisions. We need to intentionally develop the mindset and capabilities of the leader of the future. *continues* ▶

Elements of Retooling Skills to Stay Ethically Competent, con't.	How Our Thinking Needs to Change, con't.
Increasing thinking complexity	We need to be exposed to ideas, places, and experiences that are new to us in order to expand our world view. We need to continually challenge ourselves to think at higher levels of complexity and to honor increasing numbers of stakeholders as we make decisions.

What kind of leadership will it take to respond to these six trends with ethical behavior? Below, I profile this leader of the future.

Profile: The Leader of the Future

As you read the following sketch of the leader of the future, think about where you currently are in your development and what you'll need to learn in the future to be ready to lead in this broader view of leadership.

> *The leader of the future is globally aware, fast-learning, and socially and financially responsible, with amazing digital skills and social media savvy. This individual is agile, resilient, and collaborative, demonstrates exceptional thinking skills, deals well with uncertainty, has connections across disciplines, synthesizes information easily to find meaning, learns quickly and continually, adapts to solving new and complex problems, meets competing demands, is environmentally responsible, is open and transparent, and is internationally mobile, with a global view and local cultural sensitivity. This leader cares about others, behaves and leads ethically, holds people accountable while helping to develop their leadership potential, serves as a change agent promoting responsible leadership, values differences, and engages diverse collections of employees, customers, and communities in a common purpose.*[60]

It will be a stretch to be ready for all the new roles we must assume if we are to live up to this profile of the leader of the future. Here is a review of the mindset and capabilities such leaders will need.

MINDSET OF THE LEADER OF THE FUTURE:

- Has a global view and local cultural sensitivity
- Understands global expectations for ethical business and leadership
- Values differences
- Deals well with uncertainty
- Synthesizes information easily to find meaning
- Is environmentally responsible
- Is open and transparent
- Cares about others
- Is a change agent promoting responsible leadership

CAPABILITIES OF THE LEADER OF THE FUTURE:

- Treats others with care
- Collaborates using today's social media tools
- Uses systems thinking to solve complex problems
- Is socially and financially responsible
- Continually learns and adapts as the world changes
- Is agile, resilient, and collaborative
- Learns (and teaches others) how to respect each other and our differences
- Learns (quickly) across disciplines to understand a more complete picture
- Behaves and leads ethically

Serving Others Brings Out Our Best

Soren Kierkegaard said, "Don't forget to love yourself." As we imagine the kind of leadership that brings out the best in others, we must remember to care for ourselves. When we do so, we are better able to care for others.

Have you noticed how agitated you become when you forget to eat, fail to get enough rest, or forget to take breaks to do things you enjoy? Taking care of ourselves gives us a stable center from which we can more fully serve others.

In addition, when we serve others, we bring out the best in ourselves as well as those we serve. John Stuart Mill believed that in working for others, rather than ourselves, we find our own happiness:

> *Those only are happy who have their minds fixed on some object other than their own happiness; on the happiness of others, on the improvement of mankind, even on some art or pursuit, followed not as a means, but as itself an ideal end. Aiming thus at something else, they find happiness by the way.* [61]

Leaders who intentionally take the ethical leadership learning journey may also find along the way that they discover their authenticity, their best selves, and increased meaning in their work. Martin Seligman and Ed Royzman connect authenticity, morality, and happiness in this way:

> *Our theory holds that there are three distinct kinds of happiness: the Pleasant Life (pleasures), the Good Life (engagement), and the Meaningful Life. The first two are subjective, but the third is at least partly objective and lodges in belonging to and serving what is larger and more worthwhile than just the self's pleasures and desires.* [62]

Serving others is fulfilling. Individually, it improves us as leaders and connects us to a higher purpose. Organizationally, it creates the kind of meaning and engagement that releases the potential of the organization to meet its goals and to make a difference in the local and global community.

Planning for Your Ethical Leadership Future

In Part One of this book, I explored how ethical leadership is a learning journey that benefits people and organizations. I presented 7 Lenses of Ethical Responsibility that give us a multidimensional view of ethical leadership in action. In Part Two, I introduced the 14 Guiding Principles that help us honor the 7 Lenses. In Part Three, I highlighted six trends shaping the future of ethical leadership.

The next step on our journey is to ask how each of us individually will bring the 7 Lenses and the 14 Guiding Principles into our organizations and use them to guide our work. How, in fact, will we prepare ourselves to lead ethically?

Remember, ethical leadership doesn't just happen. That's why it's so important to have a plan for how to get from wherever you are now to developing the skills necessary to become an effective and ethical leader of the future.

Questions to Ask When Planning
Your Ethical Leadership Future

In the process of learning about the 7 Lenses, you may have also learned about where you are in your moral development as a leader. While we each function at different levels of thinking at different times, we can usually identify where our worldview and moral sense fall when making decisions. Ask yourself the following questions now, and then begin to build a more detailed plan for being ready.

1. How many of the 7 Lenses of Ethical Responsibility do I routinely use when making decisions?
2. What lenses of ethical leadership do I routinely leave out?
3. What experiences have led me to this way of thinking?
4. How will I need to respond to the trends in ethical business leadership I've learned about in this book?
5. How ready am I for "ethical business future?"
6. Who do I know who leads with the kind of moral responsibility that represents my next level of development?
7. How can I learn what that leader knows how to do?

8. What experiences and learning opportunities will help me practice what I need to learn?
9. How will I help other leaders prepare?

The Critical Role of the CEO in Learning the Principles and Practices of Ethical Leadership

Within businesses, individual functions may operate with their own differing views of what ethical responsibility means. The legal department may think ethical responsibility begins and ends with following laws and regulations. If so, will the CEO be able to make a compelling case for why the legal department should support the company's sustainability efforts when some aspects are not yet required by law but are considered the new global standard for doing business responsibly?

Some departments will focus primarily on one lens in daily work due to the nature of their business and their expertise. While corporate attorneys will naturally use the Law Lens, for example, the human resources department will naturally use a People Lens. Of necessity, senior leaders have the ultimate responsibility for knowing where their organization is in its ethical leadership journey and for moving it toward honoring all of what ethical leadership encompasses. This ongoing process is supported by clear and frequent communication about the organization's purpose and its ethical responsibilities.

Questions for the CEO to Ask When Building an Ethical Organization

Because successful ethical leadership incorporates different perspectives, it requires strong leadership from the CEO to pull these various perspectives together. The senior leadership perspective should be through the kaleidoscope, considering all 7 Lenses when making decisions. The CEO builds awareness of the full picture of what ethical leadership includes throughout the organization and shapes these perspectives into a coherent whole. If you are a business owner or senior leader, consider the following questions, and then build an organizational level plan for being ready for your own ethical leadership future.

1. How can I manage ethical leadership as a performance system so that I encourage and reward the kind of leadership described in this book?
2. How can I help managers throughout the organization learn to use the 7 Lenses and the 14 Guiding Principles?
3. How can I help department managers who use different lenses better listen to and learn from each other as they make decisions?
4. How will I support leaders as they take on this learning journey?
5. What additional resources will I need?
6. Which businesses can I learn from? Which businesses are doing well what I need to learn?

I believe that the 7 Lenses and 14 Guiding Principles described in this book act as keys that unlock ethical leadership. If we want to lead ethically and are willing to learn how, we will grow and improve in ways that bring out the best in ourselves and others. That, in essence, is the ethical leadership journey.

How will applying the 7 Lenses and 14 Guiding Principles transform us? When we lead with a kaleidoscopic view, we release positive energy in our organizations, with unlimited possible benefits. We become better leaders and better people. We create great places to work. We delight consumers and improve communities. We set the standard in our industries. We become part of a powerful and necessary movement. Bringing out the best in ourselves and others, we can change the world.

About Linda Fisher Thornton
and Leading in Context

Linda Fisher Thornton is founder and CEO of Leading in Context LLC, a leadership development consulting firm specializing in bringing out the best in leaders and organizations through ethical leadership. A former bank senior vice president and chief learning officer, she has been leading and training business leaders for over twenty-five years, and has worked with a wide range of clients across Fortune 500, non-profit, private practice, and university settings.

She is currently adjunct assistant professor of leadership in the University of Richmond School of Professional and Continuing Studies, where she has taught for the last twelve years. She regularly blogs and speaks about how to lead responsibly in a global society and how to build high-trust workplaces that optimize employee performance. Her Leading in Context Blog is followed by readers from 160 countries.

Thornton was named one of the 2013 Top 100 Thought Leaders in Trustworthy Business Behavior by Trust Across America and currently serves as an invited reviewer for The Millennium Project, Global Futures Study and Research, Challenges Facing Humanity #15: Global Ethics.

Leading in Context LLC is a leadership consultancy focused on developing ethical leaders and organizations. CEO and Founder Linda Fisher Thornton is leading a movement to unleash the positive power of ethical leadership in organizations. Services include consulting, training and speaking designed to develop the kind of proactive ethical leadership that transforms lives, organizations and communities. Multiple delivery methods are available including webinars, in–house *7 Lenses* training, strategic leadership retreats, aligning leadership performance systems, custom learning materials, and a subscription video series. Visit **www. LeadinginContext.com** to learn more.

Unleash the Positive Power of Ethical Leadership™

Leading in Context LLC provides clear tools for businesses of all sizes for implementing "ethical leadership future."

It is our mission to provide tools to guide you on your learning journey to ethical leadership.

14 Guiding Principles of Ethical Leadership

Lead With a Moral Compass

1. Demonstrate Personal Congruence
2. Be Morally Aware
3. Stay Competent
4. Model Expected Performance and Leadership

Lead in Ways That Bring Out the Best in Others

5. Respect Others
6. Respect Boundaries
7. Trust and Be Trustworthy
8. Communicate Openly
9. Generate Effective and Ethical Performance

Lead For the Greater Good

13. Protect Our Planet for Future Generations
14. Improve Our Global Society for Future Generations

Lead With Positive Intent and Impact

10. Think Like an Ethical Leader
11. Do Good Without Doing Harm
12. Work for Mutually Beneficial Solutions

For 7 Lenses tools, and for information about 7 Lenses consulting and training based on this book, visit **www.LeadinginContext.com**. For speaking requests and information about bulk orders, contact Info@LeadinginContext.com.

Notes and References

Opening Quotations: Dr. Rushworth Kidder, Institute for Global Ethics, in "There's Only Ethics . . ." (2001), an article based on a keynote speech he gave in 1992 to the Human Services Council of Northeast Florida.

Part 1: What Is Ethical Leadership?

1. A Learning Journey

1. Knapp, John C. (2007). *For the common good: The ethics of leadership in the 21st century.* Westport, CT: Praeger, 19.

2. There is broad agreement that the field of "leadership ethics" needs to be explored and clarified.

    Joanne Ciulla, in her 2005 article "The State of Leadership Ethics and What Lies Before Us" in *Business Ethics: A European Review*, writes, "Leadership ethics is still new and the approaches to it are quite fragmented" (323).

    Michael Brown and Linda Treviño, in the abstract of their 2006 article "Ethical Leadership: A Review and Future Directions," noted that "Ethical leadership remains largely unexplored, offering researchers opportunities for new discoveries and leaders opportunities to improve their effectiveness," 595.

    In 2009, in *Ethical Leadership: The Quest for Character, Civility and Community*, Earl Fluker wrote that "the words *ethical* and *leader* are so well entrenched in everyday speech that it is difficult to dislodge them from their popular, though largely unexamined meanings" (ix).

    O.C. Ferrell, John Fraedrich, and Linda Ferrell wrote in *Business Ethics: Ethical Decision-Making and Cases*, 2012, that "the field of business ethics continues to change rapidly as more firms recognize the benefits of ethical conduct and the link between business ethics and financial performance" (17).

141

3. Guthrie, Doug. (2012, January 31). Paying more than lip service to business ethics. Retrieved from http://www.forbes.com/sites/dougguthrie/2012/01/31/paying-more-than-lip-service-to-business-ethics/.

4. Gerzon, Mark. (2006). *Leading through conflict: How successful leaders transform differences into opportunities.* Cambridge, MA: Harvard Business School Press, 125. Gerzon is quoting from a personal interview with his sister, MIT Organization Development Consultant Jeanette Gerzon.

2. A Business Advantage

Epigraph: "Ethics and compliance risk management: Improving business performance and fostering a strong ethical culture through a sustainable process." (2007). Retrieved from http://www.ethics.org/files/u5/LRNRiskManagement.pdf, LRN, 2.

5. Ethical culture building: The modern business imperative. (2009). Waltham, MA: Ethics and Compliance Officer Association/Washington, DC: Ethics Resource Center, 20.

6. Edelman Trust Barometer. Trust has tangible benefits. Retrieved from http://www.youtube.com/watch?v=viXTQBBY258.

7. Critical elements of an organizational ethical culture. (2006) Washington, DC: Ethics Resource Center Research/Sharon, MA: Working Values, 11.

8. Josephson Institute. How to harness ethics to increase productivity. Retrieved from http://josephsoninstitute.org/business/resources/increase_productivity.html.

9. National Business Ethics Survey of Fortune 500 Employees. (2012). Washington, DC: Ethics Resource Center, 8.

10. Edelman Trust Barometer. Trust has tangible benefits. Retrieved from http://www.youtube.com/watch?v=viXTQBBY258.

11. "Ethics and compliance risk management: Improving business performance and fostering a strong ethical culture through a sustainable process." (2007). Retrieved from http://www.ethics.org/files/u5/LRNRiskManagement.pdf, 15.

12. Ethical culture building: The modern business imperative. (2009). Waltham, MA: Ethics and Compliance Officer Association/Washington, DC: Ethics Resource Center, 20.

3. 7 Lenses of Ethical Responsibility

13. Ciulla, Joanne. (2011). Ethics and leadership effectiveness. In John Antonakis, Anna Cianciolo, and Robert Sternberg (Eds.), *The nature of leadership* (302–327). Thousand Oaks, CA: Sage. 510.

14. Thornton, Linda Fisher. (2010). Leadership ethics training: Why is it so hard to get it right? Reprinted in Training and development: the best of leadership development 2006–2009. Alexandria, VA: American Society for Training and Development, 33.

15. Some states allow businesses to legally organize as Benefit Corporations, which signifies that they are held accountable for providing societal benefits that go well beyond making a profit. For more information, visit http://www.benefitcorp.net.

16. James Rouse, winner of the Presidential Medal of Freedom, quoted by Michael McCall in "A Tribute to James W. Rouse."

17. Michael Porter and Mark Kramer, Harvard University, "Creating Shared Value," *Harvard Business Review*, January–February 2011, Vol. 89, no. ½, Para. 5.

18. Aristotle, quoted on http://www.goodreads.com/author/quotes/2192. Aristotle?page=6.

Epigraph, Lens Seven: Kidder, Rushworth. (1994). *Shared values for a troubled world*. San Francisco: Jossey Bass, 3.

Part 2: 14 Guiding Principles That Honor All 7 Lenses in Daily Leadership

19. There are many possible theories and approaches to a discussion of leadership ethics. I did not limit my research to any one of them. Instead, I read widely across traditional boundaries of schools of thought. The word "research" itself, with its first known use in 1577, comes from the Old French *recerchier*, meaning "to search" (http://www.merriam-webster.com/dictionary/research), and that is what I have done. I believe, as many scholars do, that there are universal ethical principles and global values that humans share. These principles and values are not new, having been championed by philosophers and leaders from around the world, many of whom are quoted in this book. As you read this book, you may find elements of what some would describe as principle-based ethics, applied leadership ethics, character ethics, virtue ethics, value ethics, relational ethics, social ethics, utilitarianism, and environmental ethics. You may wonder what influenced my views on ethical responsibility. In early childhood, I learned about good citizenship, service, and caring for the planet at home and through actively participating in the Girl Scouts. I participated in overseas mission trips starting at the age of thirteen. At eighteen, I lived and studied abroad, becoming bilingual and comfortable in different cultures on different continents. These experiences helped shape my worldview and the broad approach I take to ethical responsibility. While I think this book transcends religious traditions in many ways, my views are grounded in a Methodist upbringing based on the work of John Wesley, who said, "Do all the good you can . . . as long as ever you can."

4. Lead With a Moral Compass

20. Some suggest that the concept of personal congruence overlaps with the Eastern philosophical concept of "inner harmony."

21. Adapted from Dieter Pauwels (2009), "Life Coaching Tips: How to Achieve Congruence," ezinearticles.com.

22. Covey, Stephen M. R. (2008). *The speed of trust: The one thing that changes everything.* New York: Free Press, 62.

23. Dr. Rushworth Kidder, Institute for Global Ethics, in his essay "There's Only Ethics," based on his keynote speech presented to the Human Services Council of Northeast Florida.

Epigraph, Principle 4: Brown, Michael, and Treviño, Linda. (2006). Ethical leadership: A review and future directions. *Leadership Quarterly,* 17, 597.

24. Berghofer, Desmond, and Schwartz, Geraldine. *Ethical leadership: Right relationships and the emotional bottom line: The gold standard for success.* Retrieved from http:// www.ethicalleadership.com/BusinessArticle.htm.

25. Brown, Jerry. (2003). Ethics in management: Setting the stage for modeling ethical behavior. Retrieved from http://www.ethics.org/resource/setting-stage-modeling-ethical-behavior, 1.

5. Lead in Ways That Bring Out the Best in Others

26. Also described as "The Ethic of Shared Reciprocity," various expressions of this fundamental moral rule can be found in tenets of most religions and creeds through the ages, testifying to its universal applicability. You can find examples and quotations at http://www.religioustolerance.org/reciproc.htm.

27. The Silver Rule is preferred by some because it avoids the Golden Rule's shortcoming of potentially advising behavior that one would prefer for oneself but that the other person does not welcome. By focusing instead on preventing harm, the Silver Rule might be seen to be consistent with the positions of Confucius and Gandhi.

28. Quotation attributed to Oliver Wendell Holmes.

29. Flew, Antony, Ed. (1979). *A dictionary of philosophy.* London: Pan Books in association with the MacMillan Press, 134 (see entry for "golden rule").

30. Manning, Rita, and Stroud, Scott. (2008). *A practical guide to ethics: Living and leading with integrity.* Boulder, CO: Westview, 241.

31. Michael Brannigan, the Pfaff Endowed Chair in Ethics and Moral Values at the College of St. Rose in Albany, NY, from his column in the Albany *Sunday Times Union,* quoted by Iowa State University, http://www.iastate.edu.

32. Hume, John. (2007). Spilling sweat, not blood: Leadership for a world without conflict. In John Knapp (ed.), *For the common good: The ethics of leadership in the 21st century.* Westport, CT: Praeger, 55.

33. Theories, Kohlberg, discussed on Richard Jacob's web page at http://www.villanova.edu.

34. Jung, Carl. (1969). Psychotherapy or the clergy. In R. F. C. Hull (Trans.), *The collected works of C. G. Jung* (vol. 11, ch. 5). Princeton, NJ: Princeton University Press.

Epigraph, Principle Seven: Josephson, Michael. (2011). Trustworthiness and integrity: What it takes and why it's so hard. Retrieved from http://josephsoninstitute.org/business/blog/2011/01/trustworthiness-and-integrity-what-it-takes-and-why-it%E2%80%99s-so-hard/.

35. Covey, Stephen M. R. (2008). *The speed of trust: The one thing that changes everything.* New York: Free Press, 2.

36. Care Theory, Western Kentucky University, http://people.wku.edu/jan.garrett/carethry.htm.

Epigraph, Principle Eight: May, Rollo. (1972). Toward new community. In *Power and innocence: A search for the sources of violence* (ch. 12). New York: Norton. http://en.wikiquote.org/wiki/Rollo_May.

37. Susan Scott addresses being well mannered and still saying what needs to be said in her book *Fierce Conversations: Achieving Success at Work & in Life, One Conversation at a Time* (New York: Viking, 2004).

38. Saint Augustine said, "It was pride that changed angels into devils; it is humility that makes men as angels," and "Humility is the foundation of all the other virtues hence, in the soul in which this virtue does not exist there cannot be any other virtue except in mere appearance" (retrieved from http://en.wikiquote.org/wiki/Augustine_of_Hippo).

Epigraph, Principle Nine: Ciulla, Joanne. (2011). Ethics and leadership effectiveness. In John Antonakis, Anna Cianciolo, and Robert Sternberg (Eds.), *The nature of leadership.* Thousand Oaks, CA: Sage, 528.

39. Pink, Daniel. (2009). *Drive: The surprising truth about what motivates us.* Retrieved from http://www.danpink.com/books/drive.

6. Lead With Positive Intent and Impact

Epigraph: Downie, Robin. (2010). Dilemmas, ethics and intent: a commentary. *Journal of Medical Ethics,* 12, 210.

40. Dr. Rushworth Kidder, Institute for Global Ethics, in "There's Only Ethics . . ." (2001), an article based on a keynote speech he gave in 1992 to the Human Services Council of Northeast Florida.

41. Maxwell, John C. (2004). *Today matters: 12 daily practices to guarantee tomorrow's success.* New York: Warner Faith, 133.

42. Baron, Jonathan. (1995). A psychological view of moral intuition. *The Harvard Review of Philosophy,* Spring, 40.

43. Victor Vroom and Arthur Jago (2007) in "The Role of the Situation in Leadership," *American Psychologist,* provide a brief history of the changes in leadership theories, beginning with the perspective that attended only to the "leader" and ignored the follower(s) and the context. In this article, they point out that "if no one is following, one cannot be leading" (17).

44. O. C. Ferrell (2004), as quoted in McMurrian, Robert C., and Matulich, Erik. (2006). Building customer value and profitability with business ethics. *Journal of Business and Economics Research*, 4(11), 11.

45. The concept that "doing good is its own reward" is also reflected in the Biblical concept that "the kind person benefits himself, but the cruel one harms himself" (Proverbs 11:17). It is no accident that almost all of the world religions have "doing good" as one of their tenets. It represents a high level of moral development.

46. Schweitzer, Albert. The discovery and meaning of reverence for life. Retrieved from http://www.albertschweitzer.info/discovery.html.

47. Ibid.

48. Patrice Sutton, MPH, consultant to the Science and Environmental Health Network, "Advancing the Precautionary Agenda," February 2009, http://www.sehn.org, 5.

49. Kunungo, Rabinda, and Mendonca, Manuel. (1996). *Ethical dimensions of leadership*. Thousand Oaks, CA: Sage, ix.

Epigraph, Preventing Harm to Constituents: Harriet Beecher Stowe, quoted from Uncle Tom's Cabin (retrieved from http://www.harrietbeecherstowecenter.org/utc/).

7. Lead for the Greater Good

Epigraph, Lead for the Greater Good: May, Rollo. (2009). *Man's search for himself.* New York: Norton, 131.

50. According to Rhett Herman, a science professor at Radford University, the earth is moving around the sun at 67,000 miles per hour, and our solar system is moving at a speed of 490,000 miles per hour (*Scientific American*, http://www.scientificamerican.com/article.cfm?id=how-fast-is-the-earth-mov). A NASA website confirms the thousands-of-miles-per-hour movement (http://image.gsfc.nasa.gov/poetry/ask/a10552.html).

51. George Washington Carver, quoted on the National Park Service website for the George Washington Carver National Monument, http://www.nps.gov/nr/travel/cultural_diversity/G_Washington_Carver_Historic_Site.html.

52. Wheatley, Margaret. (2002). It's an interconnected world. *Shambhala Sun*, April, 2.

53. Grandjean, Philippe. (2004). Implications of the precautionary principle for primary prevention and research. *Annual Review of Public Health*, 25, 199–223.

54. Ernst and Young in cooperation with GreenBiz Group. (2011). Six growing trends in corporate sustainability.

55. Herrera, Tilde. (2011). Could 2013 be a tipping point for sustainability spending? Retrieved from http://www.greenbiz.com/news/2011/05/20/could-2013-be-tipping-point-sustainability-spending, 1.

56. Trudel, Remi, and Cotte, June. (2009). Does it pay to be good? *MIT Sloan Management Review*, Winter. Retrieved from http://sloanreview.mit.edu/article/does-it-pay-to-be-good/.

Part 3: How Are Ethical Expectations Changing?

8. Getting Ready for the Future of Ethical Leadership

Epigraph, Chapter Eight: Thornton, Linda Fisher. (2010, June 14). Ethical leadership matters now more than ever. *Richmond Times Dispatch*, pp. B1.

Epigraph, 1. Broadening Scope: Andrew Crane, Professor of Business Ethics, Schulich School of Business at York University, Toronto, quoted in "Institute of Business Ethics Celebrating 25 Years" (2011), 10.

57. The Netter Principles (developed at Cornell) offer guidance about how to lead for full inclusion.

Epigraph, 2. Increased Visibility: Keith Darcy, Executive Director, Ethics and Compliance Officers Association, quoted in "Institute of Business Ethics Celebrating 25 Years" (2011), 12.

Epigraph, 3. Focus on Protecting Human Rights: United Nations Human Rights Office of the High Commissioner for Human Rights, *The Corporate Responsibility To Respect Human Rights: An Interpretive Guide*. Retrieved from http://www.ohchr.org/Documents/Publications/HR.PUB.12.2_En.pdf, 23.

Epigraph, 4. Companies Contributing to Society: Caux Roundtable Principles for Responsible Business, principle 6. Retrieved from http://www.cauxroundtable.org.

Epigraph, 5. Managing Ethics as a System: National Business Ethics Survey of Fortune 500 Employees. (2012) Washington, DC: Ethics Resource Center, 8.

58. Global guidelines for business that provide detail about the obligations of business to society include the Caux Roundtable Principles for Responsible Business, the Global Economic Ethic, the United Nations Global Compact, and the International Chamber of Commerce Charter for Sustainable Development.

Epigraph, 6. Retooling Skills to Stay Ethically Competent: Petrie, Nick. (2011). Future trends in leadership development. Greensboro, NC: Center for Creative Leadership. Retrieved from http://www.ccl.org/leadership/pdf/research/futureTrends.pdf.

59. IBM CEO study: command and control meets collaboration. (2012). Retrieved from. http://www-03.ibm.com/press/us/en/pressrelease/37793.wss.

60. Adapted from Linder Fisher Thornton, "Business Leader Future: A Sketch," originally posted on the Leading in Context blog on February 16, 2012, and compiled based on these sources:

"Key Global Trends Impacting Leadership," Hay Group press release about "Leadership 2030" report

"The Leader of the Future: Ten Skills to Begin Developing Now," Dan McCarthy, http://www.greatleadershipbydan.com

"Emerging Leadership Trends," Rick Lash, Hay Group on YouTube

"The 2020 Leader: Attributes for Success in the 2020 Workplace," Jeanne Meister at http://www.skillsoft.com

"Emerging Leadership Journeys," Spring 2011, http://www.regent.edu

"Shaping Health Systems Network: Emerging Leadership in a Global Context Center for Innovation in Health Management," UK

"Emerging Leadership Issues," Lev Lafayette, doctoral candidate at the Ashworth Centre for Social Theory

"Future Work Skills 2020," Research Institute for the Future

61. Josephson Institute Website, Quotations: "Happiness, love, life," http://www.josephsoninstitute.org.

62. Seligman, Margin, and Royzman, Ed. (2003). Happiness: The three traditional theories. Retrieved from http://www.authentichappiness.sas.upenn.edu/newsletter.aspx?id=49.

Index

for failures, 67, 68
with freedom, 108
interpersonal, 52
interpretations, 15
law as values based, 20
Lens responsibilities, 115
moral awareness and, 41, 42
Retention, 10, 89, 123
Reverence for life, 91, 103
Rewards, 10, 75, 76, 128
Right
  choices, 28
  right thing to do, 15, 21, 31
  stuck in own "rightness," 6
Rights
  basic human, 52, 95, 124–125
  property and rights boundaries, 59, 63
  respect for, 32, 53
  what you have a right to do, 15
Risk, 70, 85
Role model, 47–50. *See also* Modeling
Rouse, James, 18
Royzman, Ed, 132
Rules
  boundary rules, 60, 63
  enforcing, 60, 62
  fair play (*see* Fairness)
  Golden Rule, 52, 144n26
  harm (*see* Harm)
  Silver Rule, 52, 144n27

S

Saint Augustine, ix, [71n38], 145n38
Scarcity mentality, 96
Schwartz, Geraldine, 47
Schweitzer, Albert, 91
Scott, Susan, [71n37], 145n37
Self-interest, 42, 53, 68, 95
Seligman, Martin, 132

Senior management, 47, 60, 128–129, 134–135
Service
  caring for self, 131–132
  to community, 17, 22–23, 90, 126
  ethical leadership as service oriented, 10, 18, 80, 132
  to greater good, 107
  mindset, 86, 89, 94
  7 Lenses. *See* Lenses
Sincerity, 10, 37, 71
Skills, 43–46, 121, 128–130
Social media, 63, 72, 76–77, 123, 128–129, 131, 137
Society
  companies' responsibilities toward, 126, 147n58
  global, 107–114
  honoring societal ethics, 22–23 (*see also* Greater good)
Socrates, 37, 90
Solutions
  mutually beneficial (*see* Mutual benefit)
  oversimplified, 5, 83, 97
Special requests, fairness, 61
Speed of Trust, The (Covey), xiv, 37, 66
Stability, 37, 39, 132
Stakeholders, 14, 92, 99, 106, 122, 130. *See also* Communities; Greater good; Mutual benefit; Others; and Planet
Standards
  ethical balanced with goals, 47
  of ethical leadership, 27
  leadership conformity, 50
  respect as, 125
Status, 56, 58, 127
Stewardship, 4. *See also* Planet
Stewart, Potter, 15

Stowe, Harriet Beecher, 92
Stress as harm, 125
Stroud, Scott, 52–53
Success
  barriers to, 58, 68, 95
  connecting economic and societal, 19
  corporate openness for, 128
  credit for, 67, 68
  meaningful engagement for, 22
  support for others', 39, 55, 86
Supply chain, 18, 90, 94, 105–106
Support, 39, 53, 55, 67, 70, 80, 86
Sustainability
  bottom-line benefits of, 104
  Corporate Social Responsibility movement, 120
  Planet Lens, 17
  reverence for life, 91
  sustainable business expectations, 104–106
Sutton, Patrice, 91
Suzuki, David, 23
Synergism, business-community, 23
Synthesis of information, 4, 130, 131
Systems view, 84–87, 88, 107, 126–128, 135

T

Teams, 58, 68, 69–70
Thinking
  achievement preceded by, 80
  beyond ourselves, 6–7, 80, 84, 97, 114, 132
  broadening scope of leadership, 122